A2

ICT

for

AQA

Sharon Yull & Jackie Rogers

Series Editor – Jackie Rogers

www.heinemann.co.uk
✓ Free online support
✓ Useful weblinks
✓ 24 hour online ordering

01865 888058

Heinemann

Inspiring generations

Heinemann Educational Publishers
Halley Court, Jordan Hill, Oxford OX2 8EJ
Part of Harcourt Education

Heinemann is the registered trademark of
Harcourt Education Limited

Text © Jackie Rogers and Sharon Yull, 2004

First published 2004

09 08 07 06 05 04
10 9 8 7 6 5 4 3 2 1

British Library Cataloguing in Publication Data is available
from the British Library on request.

ISBN 0435 45486 2

Edited by Jan Doorly
Typeset and illustrated by Techtype, Abingdon

Original illustrations © Harcourt Education Limited, 2004

Cover design by Tony Richardson at Wooden Ark Ltd
Printed by Scotprint.
Cover photo: © Alamy

Acknowledgements
Every effort has been made to contact copyright holders of material reproduced in this book. Any omissions will be rectified in subsequent printings if notice is given to the publishers.

Tel: 01865 888058 www.heinemann.co.uk

CONTENTS

ACKNOWLEDGEMENTS

The authors and publisher would like to thank the following for permission to reproduce copyright material.

BSA Europe, page 63
Telegraph Group Limited, pages 60 and 76
Sanbolic, page 83
Cisco Systems Inc., page 104
Datamation, pages 105–6
International Business Machines Corporation, page 117
Computer Weekly, pages 120–1 and 129–30
Microsoft Business Solutions, pages 124–5
Tony Drewry, University of the West of England, pages 153–4 and 165
Screen shots reprinted by permission from Microsoft Corporation

Crown copyright material is reproduced under Class License No. C01W0000141 with the permission of the Controller of HMSO and the Queen's Printer for Scotland

AQA (NEAB)/AQA examination questions are reproduced by permission of the Assessment and Qualifications Alliance

Every effort has been made to contact copyright holders of material published in this book. We would be glad to hear from any unacknowledged sources at the first opportunity. Any omissions will be rectified in subsequent printings if notice is given to the publishers.

The authors and publisher would like to thank the following for permission to reproduce photographs.

Alamy: page 138
Corbis: pages 41, 49, 87, 101, 160
Epson: page 174
Getty Images: pages 56, 70, 140
Siemens: page 103

INTRODUCTION

Students embarking on the A2 portion of an A Level course in Information and Communications Technology (ICT) have spent a whole year discovering that ICT at A Level is not all about skills with packages, but has relevance to the workings of the world – in business, in finance, in the home, in manufacturing, in offices and colleges, in retail and wholesale, in fact in every aspect of modern life.

A2 ICT takes the topics studied at Advanced Subsidiary (AS) level and builds on the knowledge gathered there, to give a holistic picture of **where** ICT is used, **how** it is used, **who** provides it and **who** uses it, **why** they use it and **what** they do with it. Data processing systems, information systems and management information systems are studied: where they come from, how they are developed, and the technology required to make them effective. Organisations are studied, with respect to the technology and the systems that are used, as are corporate strategies and policies for dealing with the technology and systems, and also the different levels of working and the different information needs at these levels.

This book is aimed at A2 students following the AQA Advanced Level 6521 course. The AQA exam board has published a specification, labelled '2004 onwards', that is expected to last the lifetime of the qualification. This book has four separate sections, covering:

- A2 Unit 4 (theory module) – Information systems within organisations
- A2 Unit 5 (theory module) – Information: Policy, strategy and systems
- A2 Unit 6 (practical module) – Coursework: Use of information systems for problem solving
- Revision unit – for the two theory papers.

The first two units will follow the AQA specification closely, giving basic facts, ideas for practical exercises to apply your knowledge, quick self-test questions, and pointers on answering exam questions.

Unit 6 will explain exactly what is needed in the problem-solution coursework, and show how to produce the evidence required, giving examples at each stage.

The final revision unit will give pointers on how to read examination papers and questions, and how to interpret the question words and give the answer required. Past exam questions will be used as examples. Each A2 theory paper has an essay question, so a section on essay writing is included to aid in answering this important question.

Unit 4 covers the topics:

- Organisational structure
  - The basic concepts; the shape of and the working levels within an organisation
- Information systems and organisations

○ Data processing systems and information systems and what they are used for; what constitutes a management information system (MIS); the development and life-cycle of an information system; factors influencing the success or failure of an information system

● Corporate information systems strategy
  ○ Factors influencing how an information system is run and used within an organisation; methods and mechanisms of information flow within an organisation; levels of task and personnel within an organisation

● Information and data
  ○ Management information needs; characteristics of information; classification of information; value of information; effective presentation of information; data translation or transcription and its effect on the accuracy of the data; impact of quality and quantity of data on method of data capture

● The management of change
  ○ Factors within an organisation that need to be managed over periods of changing ICT systems

● Legal aspects
  ○ Audit requirements; disaster recovery management; risk analysis; contingency plans; impact of the implementation of legislation; ways of enforcing and controlling legislation; implications of legislation

● User support
  ○ Ways of providing user support; levels of documentation; types of training; skill updating

● Project management and effective ICT teams
  ○ Project breakdown and task allocation; characteristics of a good team

● Information and the professional
  ○ Social, moral and ethical issues for an ICT professional; codes of practice for professional organisations and ICT users; employee codes of conduct.

Unit 5 covers the topics:

● Policy and strategy issues
  ○ The need for an information technology policy; strategic implications of choices made; different users, different needs; factors influencing upgrade of technology; options for hardware and software; future proofing; back-up strategies

● Software
  ○ Procedures for software evaluation; evaluation criteria; evaluation report

● Database management concepts
  ○ Purpose of a database management system (DBMS); role of the data administrator; data consistency; data integrity; data redundancy; data independence; entity relationships; data normalisation

● Communication and information systems
  ○ Networked systems and network infrastructure; applications of communication and information systems; distributed systems; distributed databases; client/server databases

● Networks
  ○ Network security, audit and accounting; measures to protect against illegal access; audit and accounting software usage; network environments

● Human/computer interaction
  ○ Psychological factors

- Human/computer interface
  - ○ Different approaches to HCI and resource implications of creating a sophisticated HCI; customising software to create specialist HCI
- Software development
  - ○ Ways of providing software solutions for specialist applications; criteria for selection of software solution for specialist applications
- Software reliability
  - ○ Testing methods; reasons why fully tested software may fail to operate; maintenance releases
- Portability of data
  - ○ Protocols and standards for data exchange; communication standards, benefits and limitations; protocols and standards to support the World Wide Web; emergence of standards – de facto, based on historic precedent.

Unit 6 covers choosing a suitable project for use as the coursework, and gives guidelines on how to produce the solution. Notes and examples are given to help produce the:

- analysis
- design
- implementation
- testing
- evaluation
- user guide
- report.

This section also gives pointers to the accepted 'advanced' features to use in some of the more popular generic packages. It does not, however, try to be a package training manual.

The **Revision** unit covers:

- the synoptic element of A2, and the implications for revising
- exam vocabulary for A2: question words and what they are asking for
- exam technique: how to read the question and interpret what is required
- the essay question – how to approach it and answer the question to gain the most marks
- some frequently asked definitions (essential technical vocabulary)
- lists of examples, with short descriptions of where they might be used.

▲▲▲ Group activity

Before you begin your study, complete the following activity.

Preparation
If you have worked through the companion AS book, AS ICT for AQA, *you may already have this information from the activity in the Introduction.*

Write down a list of information and communication technology systems that you studied during the AS course – everyday ones, such as shop-based, home-based, banking, video hire and so on, or slightly less obvious ones such as manufacturing, aeroplane control systems, or on-line shopping.

Work in groups

Answer the questions below about five of the systems. Brainstorm your ideas and produce, in tabular form (using a particular package as directed, or one of your choice, or as a paper exercise) answers to the following questions:

- What is the context/business?
- What is the system called/what does it do (its title)?
- What kind of hardware is used for
  – data collection
  – storage
  – processing
  – output?
- What are the sources of data?
- What are the methods of entering data into the system?
- Who wrote the system, or where did it come from?
- What software was used to write the system (generic or specialist)?
- Is it part of a larger system?
- Where is information sent? How?
- Is it part of a network?
- What security is used?
- Who controls the system?
- Who operates the system?

Brainstorm in your group, and add as much of the following information as possible:

- Who uses the system?
- Is it a data processing system, an information system or a management information system?
- Who uses the output from the system?
- What type of output is it – operational, tactical or strategic?
- What levels of personnel use the system?

Whole class evaluation

Review the tables produced by other groups and suggest improvements. Try to group the systems into a set of businesses, so that you are creating a set of case studies that can be used later when applying theoretical knowledge to real situations. Amalgamate the best information and, using some form of presentation or DTP software, format it so that it makes a useful reference for later study. It could even be configured as a website and held on-line for all to read.

After you study each topic in the A2 modules, review and improve this reference work where necessary. It will form an invaluable revision aid, as most A2 exam questions are context-based.

UNIT 4:

INFORMATION SYSTEMS WITHIN ORGANISATIONS

This unit focuses on information systems and their role within organisations. You will be given an insight into information systems in terms of:

- typical life-cycles
- types of information systems
- information system strategies used within organisations
- the impact of implementing an information system and how this can bring about changes to work patterns and the working environment
- corporate IS policies and security measures.

In addition, this unit will look at the role of data and information, user support, training and codes of practice.

The chapter can be mapped through to the AQA specifications and will provide coverage of the following key areas:

- Understanding the distinction between knowledge, information and data
- Understanding the nature of data: recorded facts, events or transactions
- Understanding the different ways in which data can arise: (direct capture or as a by-product of another operation)
- Describing the effect of the quality of the data source on the information produced
- Understanding the need to encode information as data
- Understanding the problems associated with the coding of value judgements

AQA Specifications Information and Communication Technology 1999

1 Organisational structures

Organisations can be classified in many ways, according to what they do (make a product or provide a service), their motivation (to make a profit or satisfy a particular need) and in terms of how they are structured.

All organisations have a particular structure, which may be formally or informally adopted. In a formal structure there are a number of employee levels within the company which are easily recognised, so that individuals know where they are in relation to other employees in the same department, functional area or branch, and who they should report to.

An informal structure may not necessarily be clearly defined. This kind of structure is usually found in small organisations with only a handful of employees, each knowing who they should report to, without the need for an organisational chart or diagram.

1.0 Organisation charts

An organisation chart usually depicts visually the hierarchy of employees in an organisation, functional area or department, and their relationship with other employees.

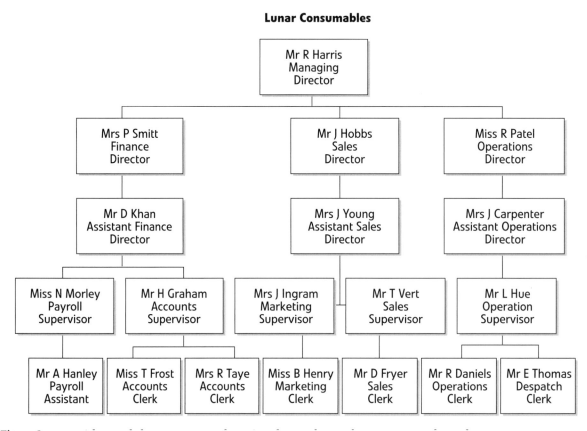

Figure 1

Basic organisational chart

An organisational chart (see Figure 1) shows:

- layers of employees from the most senior at the top to the less senior at the bottom of the structure
- names, titles and department or function for each employee/group of employees
- links depicting how each employee relates to other employees above, below and on the same level in the structure (chain of command).

Figure 1 shows:

- three functional departments: finance, sales and operations
- five defined layers of employees, extending from managing director through to clerks and an assistant
- the chain of command within the organisation
- more employees at the bottom of the structure than at the top.

 Activity 1

Based on the organisational structure shown in Figure 1, answer the following questions:

1 Which pairs of supervisors work together as co-workers and which supervisor works alone?

2 Why are there more employees at the lower levels of the structure than at the top?

3 Who would the following people need to report to in order to reach the directors of their departments?

- Miss T Frost
- Mr E Thomas
- Ms J Ingram
- Mr A Hanley

4 Why do you think that an organisational structure is needed, especially in large organisations?

1.1 Types of structure

Traditionally there are two types of organisational structures, referred to as:

- tall/hierarchical
- flat

Organisations that adopt a tall structure tend to be quite large in size. The name refers to the large number of layers in the organisation, making it tall or hierarchical. Each layer represents a level of management or function, as shown in Figure 2 on the next page.

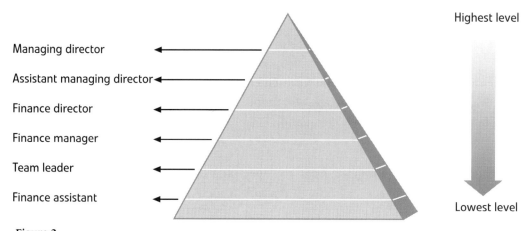

Figure 2

Tall structure

Organisational structures can also be classified as flat, as shown in Figure 3. Organisations with a flat structure tend to be smaller. They have fewer management levels.

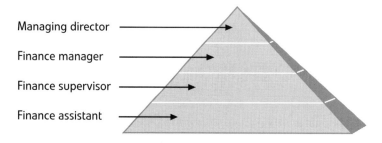

Figure 3

Flat structure

Over recent years, more organisations have chosen to adopt a flat structure because of the benefits it can bring. This transition to a less hierarchical structure is referred to as 'de-layering'. De-layering removes some of the levels of management, as shown in Figure 4, making the lines of communication between staff and management more direct.

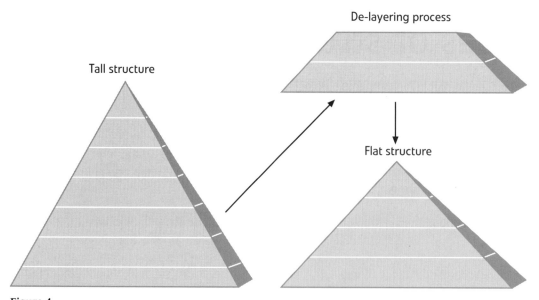

Figure 4

De-layering process

Both styles of organisational structure have benefits and drawbacks. The size of an organisation often dictates the balance of these. It would be impossible for a large multinational company to adopt a very streamlined, flat structure because of the need for co-ordination and rigour through all the management levels. Smaller organisations can be flatter because there are fewer employees, so fewer supervisors are required.

Advantages of a tall organisation structure

- Defined layers make it easier to see who is responsible for what and whom.
- There are defined functional areas, e.g. sales, finance, human resources.
- Defined management structure makes decision-making more concentrated and applicable to each level.

Disadvantages of a tall organisation structure

- Communication between the layers can be time consuming, and information can become inaccurate or misleading as it is passed on (Chinese whispers).
- Decision-making could be delayed because approval may be required from people higher up the hierarchy.
- There is a tendency for information to filter down from the top layers (top-down management) – it is manager-led and not employee-led.

Advantages of a flat organisation structure

- There is more direct communication between lower and upper levels.
- Barriers to communication are reduced.
- There is more open communication between the levels.

Disadvantages of a flat organisation structure

- Decisions and policies are dictated by one or two people, e.g. a shop manager/owner.
- Roles may not be clearly defined.
- Functional departments may not be clearly defined – a small number of people may assume a number of functional roles, e.g. in accounts, IT and sales.

What does this mean?	
Span of control:	The control that an individual has, for example a manager over a team of employees. The larger the span of control, the greater the number of employees to manage.
De-layering:	The process of reducing the number of layers in a tall structure organisation to make it flatter. The layers that are usually reduced are those of middle management.

Test your knowledge

1 Identify two basic features of an organisation structure.
2 What are the two types of organisational structure?
3 Give one advantage and one disadvantage of each type.
4 What is the process of flattening the structure of an organisation called?

2 Information systems and organisations

2.0 Information and data processing systems

Information systems are set up to manage and support the day-to-day activities of an organisation and its management. Almost every organisation will have information systems, ranging from a basic system relying on simple application software to process, store and deliver the information required, to quite complex, integrated systems that support the entire organisation. Examples of these include:

- stock control and inventory
- payroll
- invoicing
- customer accounts
- ordering and distribution.

Information systems can be classified in terms of their function and complexity. General information systems use application software tools to process, store and deliver data and information. More specific information systems are used to support a specialist function within an organisation.

2.1 General information systems

General information systems commonly use application software to support:

- databases and database management systems (DBMS)
- spreadsheets.

Databases

Databases carry out a range of functions to support all types of users. Their primary function is to store volumes of data in specific formats to allow for easy access and processing. Data in a database can be formatted to produce meaningful and useful information.

Databases offer a range of features and tools to support an organisation. Some of these are standard across a range of database software and some are more specific. Examples include:

- menu system
- security system
- input screens
  - forms
  - tables

- output screens
  - reports
  - forms
- query and filter facilities
- validation functions
- analysis tools.

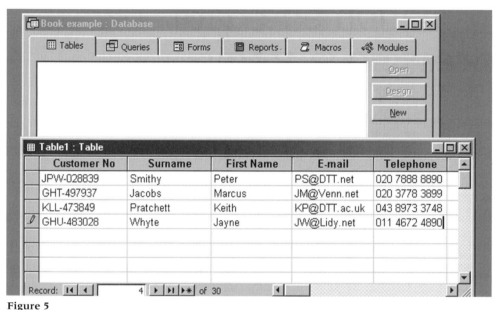

Figure 5

Example of a database table

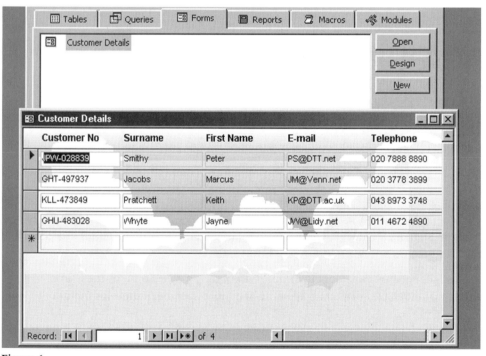

Figure 6

Example of a database form

Customer Report

Customer No	GHT-497937
Surname	Jacobs
First Name	Marcus
E-mail	JM@Venn.net
Telephone	020 3778 3899

Customer No	GHU-483028
Surname	Whyte
First Name	Jayne
E-mail	JW@Lidy.net
Telephone	011 4672 4890

Figure 7

Example of a report form

Spreadsheets

Spreadsheets meet the basic criteria of information systems because they store, process and output data items in a variety of formats. Spreadsheets are commonly used to model numerical and financial data. Examples of their use include profit-and-loss accounts, monthly forecasting, expenditure and salary sheets. Spreadsheets have a range of functions including:

- automatic calculations
- modelling and predictive facilities
- graphical outputs
- programming functions
- automatic updating.

	Jan	Feb	Mar	Apr	May	June	
Income	£	£	£	£	£	£	
Wages	620	620	620	620	620	620	
Expenses							
Entertainment	110	130	115	90	100	75	
Car tax	20	20	20	20	20	20	
Eating out	40	60	20	40	35	30	
Clothes	150	220	100	120	135	170	
Subtotal	320	430	255	270	290	295	
Balance	300	190	365	350	330	325	

Figure 8

Monthly expenditure spreadsheet

Spreadsheets provide a clear and consistent worksheet format that helps you understand and interpret the data. Data can be typed in and stored as a skeleton template, and further updates can then be added. Provided that formulas have been set up on the spreadsheet, new data can be incorporated and updated easily, giving the user current facts and figures.

A spreadsheet containing large volumes of data may not be easy to interpret, however. Some spreadsheet applications have built-in chart and graphical facilities to provide a visual interpretation of data. Examples of these can be seen in Figure 9.

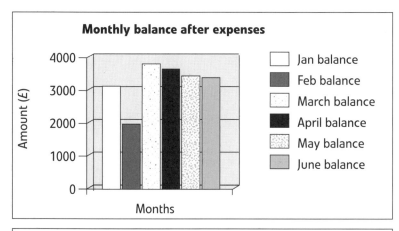

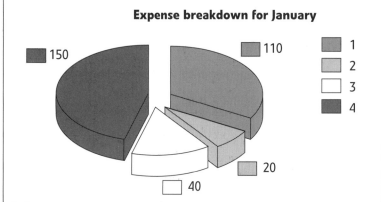

Figure 9

Examples of the charts and graphs offered by spreadsheets

Test your knowledge

1 What is meant by a general information system?
2 Give two examples of general information systems.
3 How could these systems be used to help an organisation?

2.2 Specific information systems

Databases and spreadsheets are two examples of general information systems that can assist organisations in their pursuit of manageable and supportive data systems. However, more specific information systems also exist.

Examples of these include:

- strategic level systems
- management level systems
- knowledge level systems
- operational level systems.

Each of these information system types supports various aspects of an organisation, from strategic and tactical levels down to operational levels. Specific information systems can also be integrated into functional areas of an organisation – for example there may be a sales information system or a finance information system.

Information systems can be classified as shown in Figure 10.

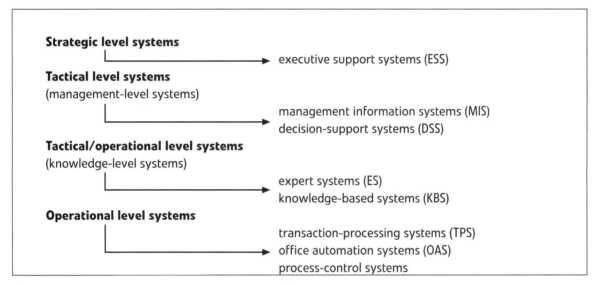

Figure 10

Types of specific information system

Strategic level systems

This level of information system supports senior executives in making unstructured decisions at a strategic level. The types of decisions which will be made include:

- Should we consider diversifying into new markets?
- Should we make a bid to acquire new businesses?
- How could we embrace new challenges in the area of e-commerce?

Strategic level information systems are set up to forecast, budget and plan for the future, extending over a long-term period of five years or more. Specific information systems can be set up, for example an **executive support system** (ESS).

Executive support systems support staff at a strategic level, and their function is to provide the guidance needed to carry out long-term forecasting and planning. These systems use current data and information in order to establish trends or anomalies which can then be used for future planning. For example, an organisation that wishes to transfer production to continental Europe over the next five years may look at a range of available data sources, including:

- cost of manufacturing (labour, transportation, premises)
- import and export issues (cost, barriers to trade)

- existing businesses already trading in Europe and their profitability
- current financial status and whether there would be enough capital to finance such a venture in the future
- existing competition in Europe.

In order to identify specific trends, an ESS may rely on historical data to identify what has been done in the past and whether it was successful.

A successful ESS will have the following characteristics:

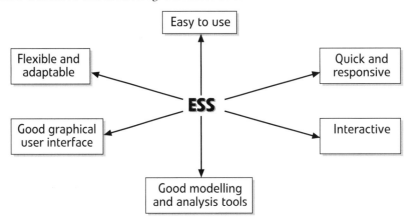

Users who will be accessing an ESS may have very limited IT knowledge or skills. Senior executives will not necessarily be technically orientated and therefore access to an ESS must be easy and quick. The information required should be produced by the ESS within a specified time period to enable decisions to be made quickly.

An ESS must be able to interact easily and effectively with other systems in order to retrieve the data required. For example, decisions on whether to take over a new company may require the ESS to retrieve share price data from an external database such as the London Stock Exchange. In order to facilitate correct decisions, the modelling and analytical tools should be first class and the graphical user interface (GUI) should be easy to use and informative.

Finally, an ESS has to be flexible and adaptable in order to support the ever-changing needs of an organisation.

Management level systems

Management level systems are designed to support middle management at the tactical level, in making unstructured and semi-structured decisions, at a lower level than those offered by strategic level systems. These systems support management levels within an organisation but they are not exclusive to managers. Other information systems may be included:

- management information systems
- operational information systems.
- decision support systems

Management information systems (MIS) support management at all levels within an organisation by providing them with data and information based on both current and historical records, from which informed and detailed decisions can be made. An MIS is typically based on internal data. Examples of this include:

- financial status
- weekly, monthly, and quarterly forecasts and trend analysis
- performance and productivity levels
- sales targets and figures.

The primary role of an MIS is to convert data from internal and external sources into information, so that it can be communicated to all levels within an organisation. Management will use the information to enable them to make more effective decisions.

Decision-support systems also support managers, helping them to make decisions that are characterised as being semi-structured or unstructured. A DSS has to be inherently dynamic in order to support the demand for up-to-date information, giving a fast response to the changing conditions of an organisation.

A DSS is a complex analytical system that includes a variety of analysis and modelling tools to enable managers to enquire about, process and evaluate data.

Knowledge level systems

Knowledge level systems are, by definition, specialist systems that provide support for knowledge users within an organisation. This type of information system is not confined to a specific user or a specific decision type.

The function of a knowledge information system is to assist an organisation in its quest to identify, analyse, integrate and collaborate on new ideas and information in order to be more efficient or profitable, or to ensure high quality standards in services and/or products.

Knowledge level system users are generally those who have high academic status or are professionals such as engineers, doctors, lawyers and scientists. Their role within the organisation would be to seek out technical facts, information and knowledge, which can then be analysed, processed and integrated into the organisation.

Examples of how knowledge level systems can be used in a hospital include:

- identifying patients who are more at risk of certain medical conditions
- measuring the impact of certain drugs on particular categories of patients
- monitoring medical histories.

There are many ways in which data can be extracted to provide the information required for analysis. Some are quite straightforward and involve the sorting or filtering of information using conventional application software. However, the specific tools and techniques known as expert systems and data mining are also available.

Expert systems are an advanced type of knowledge-level system. Expert systems encapsulate the experience and specialised knowledge of experts and relay this information to non-experts, so that they too can have access to specialist knowledge.

Expert systems are based on a reasoning process that resembles human thought processes. Rules and reasoning processes have been extracted by experts in the field. An example of their use is for patient diagnosis.

Data mining is a generic term that covers a range of technologies. The 'mining' of data refers to the extraction of information through tests, analyses and sets of rules. Information will be sorted and processed from a data set in order to find new information or data anomalies.

Data mining embraces a wide range of technologies including rule induction, neural networks and data visualisation, all working to provide the analyst with a better understanding of the data.

What does this mean?

Rule induction:	In expert systems, a conditional statement that tells the system how to react to a particular situation.
Neural networks:	A type of artificial intelligence that attempts to imitate the way a human brain works. Rather than using a digital model, which manipulates zeros and ones, a neural network works by creating connections between *processing elements*, the computer equivalent of neurons. The organisation and weights of the connections determine the output. Neural networks are particularly effective for making predictions when networks have a large database of examples to draw on.
Data visualisation:	Transforming numeric and textual information into a graphic format. Visualisations are used to explore large quantities of data in order to understand trends or principles.

Operational level systems

This level of information system supports operational managers and supervisors and assists them by tracking and monitoring activities at this level.

The relevant types of activities include:

- processing sales figures for a set period
- setting production and productivity levels
- examining daily work flow.

Operational level systems will provide answers to structured questions and aid decisions where there are a limited number of outcomes, such as:

- how much is being produced of an item, or in a time frame
- how many items are in stock
- when production targets will be met based on current workflow levels.

For example, if the question is 'How many items are in stock?', a report such as the one below could be generated.

Stock report at 1 March 2004			
Stock number	**Stock item**	**Quantity**	**Location**
RT1244000	Fan belt	136	Aisle 6B
Y45501	Spark plug	26	Aisle 2A
FG2670911	Fuse	12	Aisle 1D
HI611098	Washer	180	Aisle 1B

Within the operational level category there are three different types of information system:

- transaction-processing systems (TPS) or data-processing systems (DPS)
- office automation systems (OAS)
- process-control systems.

A **transaction-processing system** supports the operational level of organisations by providing answers for structured, routine decisions. Such systems are pivotal to any organisation because they provide the backbone for day-to-day activities and a basis for other information support sysems including MIS. Examples include holiday-booking systems, customer ordering systems and payroll systems.

A TPS/DPS carries out the essential role of gathering, collating and processing the daily transactions of an organisation. Typical functions include:

- accounts
- stock management
- invoicing
- ledger keeping.

A TPS/DPS has pre-specified functions – the decision rules and output formats cannot easily be changed by the end user. These systems are directly related to the structure of an organisation's data.

Office automation systems are set up to identify ways of increasing levels of efficiency and productivity. Various tools and software are available to schedule, monitor and improve work flows. An OAS will enable staff to:

- communicate more effectively
- promote collaborations and group synergy
- structure daily tasks and activities
- track and schedule appointments and activities
- increase productivity by automating repetitive tasks.

Office automation systems can be quite simple, drawing on the functions of application software such as word processors, spreadsheets, databases, and communications software such as e-mail.

More complex software tools can also be used to focus on a specific area of workflow or productivity, such as document imaging, workflow-management systems, or electronic document-management systems.

Process-control systems monitor, support and control certain process activities in a manufacturing environment. Applications supporting process-control systems can help an organisation to:

- improve quality control
- improve designs
- identify development status or stage in the product life-cycle.
- plan projects
- identify resource requirements

A wide range of software is available to support both general and specific activities under process-control systems, as shown in the table.

Software type	Function
Spreadsheet	■ Costing of manufacturing items ■ Forecasting sales ■ Identifying break-even and profit margin points ■ Analysing work patterns and efficiency levels
Statistical packages	■ Examining productivity levels to identify optimum working conditions ■ Identifying relationships between workforce and productivity
Project management	■ Gantt charts identifying timings of activities ■ Scheduling tasks and activities ■ Identifying task dependencies
Computer-aided design (CAD)	■ Interactive development of drawings and designs ■ Professional drafting
Computer-aided manufacture (CAM)	■ Controlling production equipment more accurately ■ Integrating with other manufacturing systems ■ Ensuring quality procedures

2.3 Role of information systems in decision-making

In every organisation, decisions are made on a daily basis. These decisions are taken at various levels and are of varying complexity.

In a typical organisation, there are three levels of management, each representing a different decision type, as shown in Figure 11.

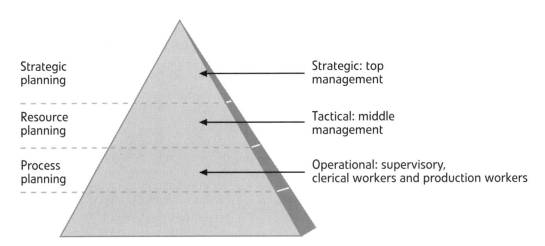

Figure 11

Levels and types of decision-making

The strategic level represents the highest layers of management – usually a managing director, chief executive and senior managers. Decisions at this level encompass planning for the future, strategic decisions such as mergers and take-overs, and forecasting markets and trends.

The tactical level represents middle management, including heads of department and assistant directors. The decisions here focus on project plans, resource issues and financing.

The operational level concentrates on day-to-day decision-making, and the basic functioning of the organisation. This level includes the majority of the workforce.

Decisions can also be classified according to their nature – they can be referred to as structured, semi-structured or unstructured decisions. **Structured** decisions are routine and there will be a set procedure for arriving at them. **Unstructured** decisions require judgement and evaluation, and involve a situation for which there is no pre-existing set of rules or guidelines.

Most structured decisions will be taken at the operational level, and most unstructured decisions will be at the strategic and tactical levels, as shown in Figure 12.

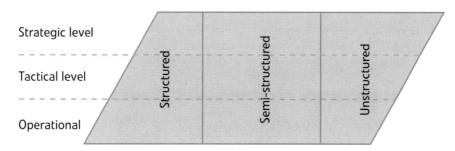

Figure 12

Distribution of structured and unstructured decisions in an organisation

Impact of information systems on decision-making

The decision-making process produces a response or action. Decisions at all levels are made on a day-to-day basis – some can be made by an individual, others by teams of people; they can use statistics, facts, knowledge, and historical and forecast data.

Information systems can support managers at all levels with the decision-making process. They can be used to:

- analyse facts and figures
- provide analytical, forecasting and modelling tools
- provide diagnosis and value judgements
- identify trends, patterns and anomalies within data sets.

Some specific information systems can be used to make decisions beyond the capacity of the people involved. For example, expert systems have their own built-in knowledge base that can be used to support non-experts in their decision-making process.

Test your knowledge

1. Identify the three types of decisions and explain the characteristics of each.
2. How does each decision type fit within the levels of an organisation?
3. How can information systems be used to support managers in the decision-making process?
4. Give an example of an information system that has its own knowledge base and can be used to support non-experts in their decision-making.

Activity 2

Fill in the gaps in the table below.

Decision type	Example of decision	Department/personnel
Structured	Whether a widget passes quality control	Operative working in a factory making widgets
Semi-structured		Help desk clerk in an IT department
	Whether to take on extra staff members in finance department	Middle manager in finance department
Unstructured		Managing director of a large retail outlet
	Whether to place another stock order	Stock clerk in distribution department
Structured	When to process customer orders for the day	

2.4 Definition of a management information system

Management information systems summarise and report on the basic operations of an organisation. An MIS converts data from a variety of internal and external sources, usually via a transaction-processing system (TPS), and presents the output information in an appropriate format such as a report that can be used by managers at different levels.

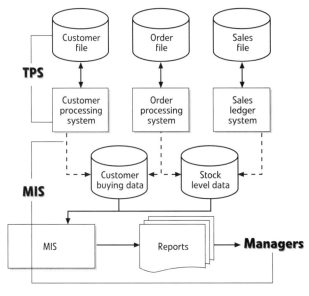

Figure 13

MIS input, conversion and output system

Management information systems are used to support tactical and strategic decision-making and are therefore associated with management at these levels. An MIS can embrace a range of information systems including:

- information reporting systems
- decision-support systems
- executive information systems.

In order to assist managers in their decision-making, data and information need to be available in an appropriate format. **Information reporting systems** meet this purpose. Reports can be generated periodically at predetermined intervals (e.g. every hour, day, week or month), on demand – as and when required – or by exception when an event triggers the need for a report.

The report will use data collected internally and possibly externally at an operational level.

Report type	Internal data	External data
Stock requisition	Current stock levels and stock prices (generated by warehouse or stock personnel)	Availability and pricing of stock items (suppliers)
Productivity	Number of widgets made in a set period, number of personnel making the widgets and cost of production	Competitors' widget output levels, market share information

Decision systems or **decision-support systems** (DSS) provide managers with the knowledge and information needed to support semi-structured or unstructured decisions.

A DSS should:

- provide support for semi-structured and unstructured decisions
- be integrated across operational, tactical and strategic levels of decision-making
- support all phases of the decision-making process
- be easy to use.

The way in which a DSS works is to mimic the way human experts would go through the process of decision-making. Using tools and software such as artificial intelligence, fuzzy logic, data mining, knowledge-based systems, neural networks and heuristics, the DSS will build up a knowledge base to support the decision-making process.

What does this mean?

Fuzzy logic: A type of logic that recognises more than simple true and false values. With fuzzy logic, propositions can be said to have degrees of truthfulness. For example, the statement 'Today is sunny' might be 100% true if there are no clouds, 80% true if there are a few, 50% true if there are many, and 0% true if it rains all day.

Heuristics: Common-sense rules drawn from experience.

The function of **executive information systems** (EIS) is to provide analytical, comparative and forecast tools for effective strategic decision-making. An EIS is designed to support senior managers, but information may be generated at an operational level.

Test your knowledge

1 What is the function of an MIS?
2 What types of information systems does the term MIS embrace?
3 Which types of decisions should a decision-support system (DSS) support?
4 How does a DSS work?
5 What level of decision-making is an executive information systems (EIS) designed to support?

Activity 3

Most organisations have MIS support. Carry out some research to identify an organisation that uses an MIS system, and answer the following questions.

1 What is the role of the MIS within the organisation?
2 What specific areas or functions does the MIS target and support?
3 What system was in place before the MIS (if any)?
4 Prepare a short report on the MIS system and present it orally to your group.

2.5 The development and life-cycle of an information system

All systems evolve, and the majority of systems show a similar pattern or life-cycle. The systems life-cycle is a well-established way of planning an information system, based on a number of stages with a beginning, a middle and an end. For information system development, the traditional life-cycle has six stages:

1 project definition
2 systems study
3 design
4 programming
5 installation
6 post-implementation.

Each stage consists of a set of activities that must be performed before moving onto the next stage.

Figure 14 shows two models of an information system life-cycle. There are a number of similarities between the two – each model performs similar tasks at each stage of development. The first model (on the left) is very characteristic of the systems life-cycle. The second, on the right, represents the general six-stage information system model.

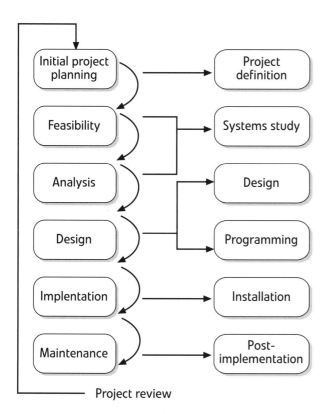

Figure 14

Comparative life-cycle models

Project definition

The first stage of an information system life-cycle is that of project definition. Project definition attempts to answer questions such as:

- Why is a new system required?
- What are the objectives for the new system proposal?
- How do we integrate the new system?

This stage identifies whether a problem exists and how it can be solved by a revised or new information system.

This stage also looks at the scope and objectives of the project. Setting the scope identifies which areas within an organisation are to be involved with new system development. The areas could be identified functionally (such as sales, finance or IT) or by specialism (such as pensions, insurance or mortgages).

Systems study

The systems study stage analyses the problems identified with the existing system and sets out objectives for overcoming them. Solutions are identified and analysed in terms of feasibility. The five main feasibility factors are known as TELOS: for technical, economic, legal, operational and schedule feasibility.

- Technical feasibility – possible technical problems and the different solutions needed to address them
- Economic feasibility – the costs and benefits of implementing a new system

- Legal feasibility – what legal issues may arise and possible ways to address them
- Operational feasibility – how the introduction of the new system will affect day-to-day processes
- Schedule feasibility – scheduling issues and the steps needed to resolve them.

At this stage facts and information about the organisation, the existing system and the proposed system are all gathered. This stage is sometimes referred to as the fact-finding stage, where techniques such as interviewing, observation, investigation of documents and questionnaires are all used to determine the framework for the new system and the remainder of the project life-cycle.

Design

The design stage produces the logical and physical specification for the new system proposal. The design stage may include the use of specific tools and techniques such as data flow diagrams, structure diagrams and flow charts to provide a clear overview of the design.

Programming

The programming stage interprets the designs and translates these into appropriate software program code, if applicable.

Installation

The installation stage brings together the completed designs and looks at any final modifications that are needed to make the new system fully operable. Considerations might include testing, training and conversion procedures. Final checks are made to ensure that everything works.

Post-implementation

Post-implementation examines the system and evaluates its performance after a set period. The evaluation will check to see whether the system has complied with the original objectives, and whether any further adjustments need to be made.

Other development models

These stages within a system's life-cycle are commonly recognised, and feature prominently in other models used to design and build information systems. Other development models include:

- the waterfall model
- rapid applications design (RAD)
- the spiral model
- dynamic systems development methodology (DSDM).

The **waterfall model** is based on a series of steps that should be addressed when building an information system. The order of these steps is predefined, with a review at the end of each.

The sequence of phases in the waterfall model can be seen in Figure 15.

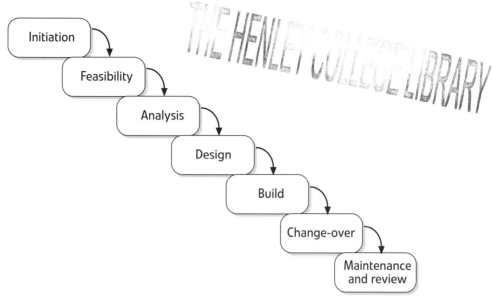

Figure 15

Waterfall model

Rapid applications development (RAD) uses prototyping to develop information systems. Prototyping involves building a model of the new system in order to evaluate it and pinpoint necessary changes before doing the detailed work of building the entire system. It has the benefit of achieving a faster development time compared to more traditional methodologies.

The **spiral model** is an iterative (repeating) systems development model based on four main activities. These are:

- planning
- risk analysis
- engineering
- customer evaluation.

This model was developed in response to the fact that systems development projects tend to repeat the stages of analysis, design and code as part of the prototyping process.

Dynamic systems development methodology is based on the principles of rapid applications development. Put together by the DSDM Consortium, DSDM is a more up-to-date version of RAD. The aim is for new information systems to be built more in line with the needs of users.

Information system building must follow a formal procedure or life-cycle approach in order to ensure consistency, quality and overall success. However, the systems life-cycle approach is costly and can be time-consuming in terms of collecting sufficient evidence before proceeding to the next stage.

Test your knowledge

1 What are the six stages in the life-cycle of an information system?
2 What sort of questions could be asked in the project definition stage?
3 What do you think are the advantages of using a life-cycle approach to information system building?
4 Why does each stage need to be complete before moving onto the next?
5 Are there any disadvantages to using a life-cycle approach?

Activity 4

You have been asked by the owner of a small DVD and games shop to design an automated system to help with day-to-day operations and replace the existing manual one. The system design could be for one of the following areas:

■ stock control
■ accounts
■ storage of members' details and new memberships.

1 Using one of the life-cycle models, outline what you would do in each of the stages for one of the systems.

2 What information would you need to help you with the design?

3 How would you implement the new system, taking into consideration that a manual system already exists? Justify your reasoning.

2.6 Success or failure of a management information system

Not all management information systems achieve their function of supporting managers in the decision-making process. A number of factors can influence the success or failure of an information system, as shown in Figure 16.

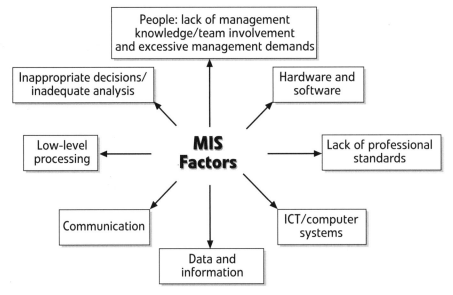

Figure 16

Factors affecting the success or failure of an MIS

People: lack of management/team involvement

People's expertise and co-operation are needed for the design, information input, manipulation and maintenance of an MIS. The MIS is only as good as the expert whose knowledge has been drawn upon, and if management have not been fully engaged with the design of the MIS the completed system may not meet the requirements of the end user. People are also needed to interrogate the MIS and ensure that the correct information is output.

Hardware and software

An MIS should be flexible enough to cope with both current and future demands. The hardware and software used to support the MIS should be sufficiently dynamic to meet these demands.

The functions of an MIS range from reporting to decision-making and offering executive support. The software needs to be:

- analytical
- intelligent
- predictive
- user friendly.

The hardware and the software need to be sophisticated enough to process data at all levels, draw upon the stored MIS knowledge base to make informed value judgements, and output the information in an appropriate format.

Lack of professional standards

Lack of or neglect of professional standards at any level can result in the failure of an MIS. If personnel are not operating to agreed standards the MIS can become prone to errors and inconsistencies.

ICT systems

The ability of an MIS to interact with and transfer data to other ICT systems also contributes to the success or failure of the system. Information that is input into the MIS may be generated from other systems at a lower operational level, so compatibility of systems is paramount. Also, once the information has been processed the MIS may need to transfer the knowledge onto other systems and to users at tactical and strategic levels.

Data and information

The sources of the data and information that feed into an MIS will have a direct impact on the quality and reliability of the output data.

To ensure that the output data is delivered at the correct level and in the appropriate format, the source data needs to be clear, concise and easily accessible.

Communication

Good communication is paramount to the success of an MIS. Communication with system commissioners, management and end users is required from the initial design through to data input, processing, storage and output.

Good communication is also needed to ensure that the correct data and information are being gathered. This information could be generated across all three levels of an organisation – operational, tactical and strategic. The need for good teamwork and standards to ensure consistency in the design and implementation process of the MIS should also be communicated throughout each management level.

Low-level processing

Within an organisation a number of processing activities take place at all levels. Concentration on low-level processing tasks and decisions could result in a system being built (at great cost) that is not supportive of tactical and strategic users.

Inadequate analysis and inappropriate decisions

If sufficient time has not been set aside during the development stages of an MIS, the analysis may have been inadequate and inappropriate decisions may have been taken. Insufficient gathering of evidence and interaction with end users could result in the building of a system that does not match the requirements of the end users or the needs of the organisation.

 Test your knowledge

1 What are the factors that can contribute to the success or failure of an MIS?
2 Why do you think that an MIS needs to be flexible?
3 Identify three functions of an MIS.

 Activity 5

Carry out research to find an organisation that has implemented an MIS. For that organisation identify:

1 Whether the implementation of the MIS was a success or failure.
2 Whether the MIS meets the original expectations and objectives.
3 Why the MIS is a success or failure.
4 Which areas of the MIS could have been improved (if any).

Exam questions

1 **(a)** Describe what is meant by a management information system (MIS). *(2 marks)*

   (b) Explain why an organisation would implement an MIS. *(3 marks)*

   AQA June 2003

2 Information is communicated at three levels within an organisation. State these **three** levels. *(3 marks)*

   AQA Jan 2003

3 Describe what is meant by the following terms, and give an example of each:

   (a) data processing system *(3 marks)*

   (b) a management information system *(3 marks)*

   AQA Jan 2003

4 A company which distributes car parts has recently expanded and wants to commission a new corporate information system. It needs the system to be successful to ensure the future growth of the business.

   State **five** factors that could cause failure of such an information system. *(5 marks)*

   AQA June 2002

3 Corporate information systems strategy

3.0 Factors influencing information systems

It is recognised that a number of factors can impact upon the development and growth of an information system in an organisational environment. These factors broadly cover three main areas: human resources, organisational culture, and current and required IT resources.

Human resources

The main areas where human resources can affect the development of a system are:

- standards and behavioural factors, such as personalities, motivation and ability to adapt and change
- responsibility for the information system within the organisation.

Human resources are required to manage and maintain the data that supports the information system, and the decision-making process that is pivotal to strategic-based systems.

The design of information systems also depends on the knowledge and skills of the staff who manage, program, analyse and implement the technology. Depending upon how many people have had input into the overall design, issues of ownership may have an impact on the functionality of the information system by restricting its use, for example, to certain levels of management within the organisation.

Organisational culture and environment

The culture of an organisation can have a profound impact upon information systems and how they are received. The following are the important factors:

- organisations and functions of management
- methods of planning and decision-making
- legal and audit requirements
- general organisation structure
- information flow.

Some organisations are quite reluctant to introduce new technology. Embracing new ways of doing things and being open to change is challenging, and conservative attitudes can impact upon the development and use of an information system.

Some levels of management within an organisation may not see the benefits of using an information system. The cost and time required to fully implement a system of this nature may be considered to outweigh the long-term gains.

Certain management styles can also impact upon information systems in organisations. Traditionally there are three types of management style:

- technical-rational
- behavioural
- cognitive.

A **technical-rational** style of management produces a mechanistic approach to operations. An organisation adopting this style will be closed to the idea that the information system can continually improve operations, productivity and efficiency levels.

A **behavioural** style of management is more open, flexible and adaptable. People are considered to be pivotal to the success of the organisation and therefore an information system would be used to support the various levels within an organisation in the functions of planning and decision-making.

The **cognitive** approach promotes an organisational culture built around 'knowing' and 'learning'. Therefore the role of an information system would be to extract knowledge and use this to support non-experts in a particular area.

Current and required IT resources

An information system may be developed around an organisation's existing hardware and software provision. If this provision is inadequate, outdated, too slow or incompatible with other systems, for example, the information system will be working to the same poor standards and may inherit the same problems.

If no provision has been made to update the hardware or software, the information system will remain static and will not be able to develop and expand to take on more processing, decision-making or knowledge-based tasks in the medium to long term.

Other factors

Other factors that can influence information systems development include the way in which raw data is collected, the type of processing activity, cost and time issues, and dependency on human operators and designers. To ensure that information systems are used at optimum levels, a balance of all of these resources needs to be considered.

Test your knowledge

1 Which factors can influence the performance of an information system within an organisation?

2 Why can an organisation's culture impact upon information systems?

3 What are the three types of management style?

4 What are the differences between the three?

5 Why can an organisation's existing hardware and software impact upon the performance of an information system?

3.1 Information flow

Information flow within an organisation can be influenced by a number of factors, including:

- size and structure of the organisation
- information type/nature
- tools for delivering information
- source and receiver.

The **size and structure** of an organisation can have a profound effect on how easily and quickly information flows within it. Section 1 examined different types of organisational structure – flat and tall/hierarchical, with the relative merits and drawbacks of each (pages 6–9).

In terms of information flow, organisations with a tall structure could provide a better environment because they have clear divisions into functional or specialist departments such as sales or finance. The information flow could be more direct and therefore the speed of communication could be that much quicker.

In a smaller organisation with a flatter structure, information flowing into and out of the organisation may be slower, as no one person would be directly accountable.

The **nature of the information** will also influence the effectiveness of communication within an organisation. Formal information, such as the passing of a customer order from sales to despatch, may be deemed to be a priority, resulting in a quicker flow of information. Internal communications such as the announcement of the next team briefing, however, may be passed on with less urgency.

The **tools for delivering information** can be an important factor, and ICT can help to disseminate information quickly and effectively. For example, if the warehouse staff wanted to check current stock levels and pass this information onto the ordering department, they could track current levels on a computer system and generate a report, as opposed to physically checking the stock levels.

The flow of information within an organisation is very dependent on the **source and receiver** of the information. Both sender and receiver can be human or electronic. The source needs to be accurate and relevant, and the receiver needs to react to the information, process it and respond in a timely fashion.

Once information has been received, recipients can respond in a number of different ways. They (or the system) can pass on the information, making them both a receiver and a sender. They or the system can also carry out an action as a result of the information received, therefore activating a process. Alternatively on receipt of the information they or the system could do nothing, retaining the information and storing it in their own memory bank. Figure 17, on the next page, shows these actions in diagrammatic form.

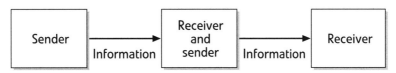

Information is sent to the receiver, who then passes it on to a third party. The recipient thus has a dual role as receiver and sender.

Information is sent to the receiver, who then carries out an action and processes the information received.

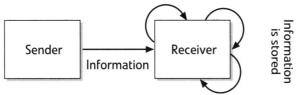

Information is sent to the receiver, who stores it in a memory bank

Figure 17

Information transmission and storage

Information flow within an organisation can be tracked easily through the use of specified tools and techniques. Figure 18 shows the components of an information flow diagram.

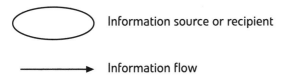

Figure 18

Information flow diagram components

Such diagrams provide a simple overview of how information is routed between different parts of an organisation, and also how information is communicated between the internal and external aspects of an organisation. For example, a customer placing an order with the sales department instigates a certain pattern of information flow (see Figure 19).

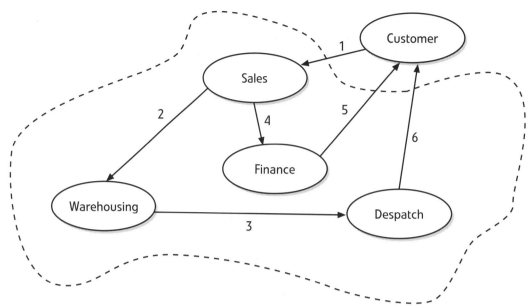

Information flows:

1 Order request
2 Picking list
3 Order details
4 Customer details
5 Invoice
6 Customer order

Figure 19

Information flow diagram

Information flows can be categorised as **formal** or **informal** depending upon the type of sender, the receiver and the message that is being transmitted. Formal information flows may include the following examples:

- between department managers discussing marketing and promotion strategies
- a manager informing a supervisor about staff redundancies
- a supervisor informing his or her team about the implementation of an ICT network.

Formal information flow follows set procedures to ensure that the information reaches the correct person. For example, agendas are distributed for team meetings, and minutes are e-mailed to all who attended. Both documents are stored in a file. Informal information flows tend to be at a more operational level, with the transfer of general information such as the date of the Christmas party. This type of information may be passed on through conversation or informal notes.

Test your knowledge

1 What factors can influence the flow of information within an organisation?
2 Why could a tall organisation structure promote a better information flow?
3 Do you think that ICT helps or hinders information flow within an organisation? Fully justify your answer.
4 What can happen to information when it is passed between two or more parties?
5 Give four examples of an information flow within an organisation.

Activity 6

1 Complete five possible information transfers on an information flow diagram like the following.

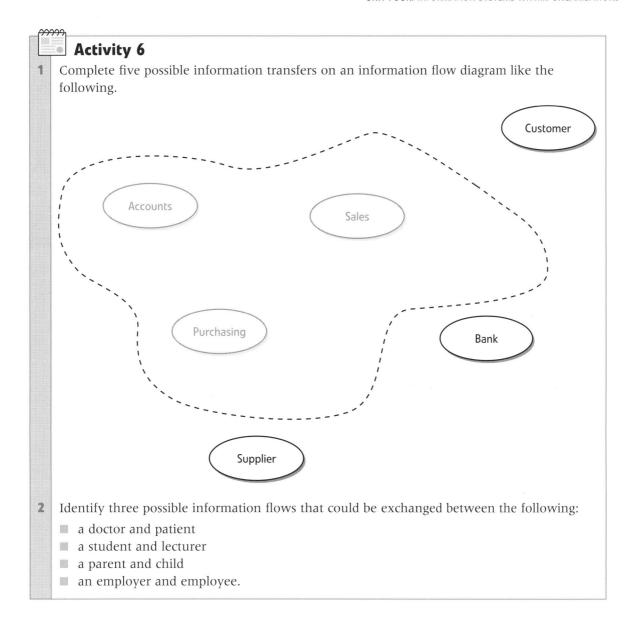

2 Identify three possible information flows that could be exchanged between the following:
- a doctor and patient
- a student and lecturer
- a parent and child
- an employer and employee.

3.2 Personnel

In any medium to large organisation there will be distinct layers of personnel ranging from operatives, clerks and administrators to supervisors, middle management, senior executives and directors.

Personnel within an organisation each carry out a specific role or roles, and these roles dictate their requirements from an information system.

Personnel at the **strategic** level of an organisation include:

- managing directors
- chair persons
- chief executives
- branch managers or senior managers.

Their work impacts upon the entire organisation, as they will be involved with high-level decision-making and strategy planning.

Typical decisions assigned at a strategic level include:

- how much money to invest into a venture
- take-over and merger policy involving other organisations
- diversification of a product range (whether to branch out into other areas)
- re-location of branches
- forward planning, including resource and staff issues – redundancies, recruitment and so on.

At the **tactical** or implementation level of an organisation, personnel could include:

- department/section managers
- assistant managers
- supervisors
- team/section leaders.

At this level personnel would be expected to manage and supervise their own section within an organisation. Their span of control would be restricted to a team of employees.

Typical tasks assigned at a tactical or implementation level would include:

- compiling staffing rotas
- putting together management reports for senior management on costs, resources and productivity/efficiency levels
- motivating their team
- day-to-day supervision of the team's tasks and responsibilities.

At the **operational** level, employees and job roles would be focused more on day-to-day processing tasks. Typical employees would include:

- clerks
- administrators
- support staff
- operators
- manual workers/labourers.

At this level workers are focused more on the physical or intellectual aspects of getting a task done, such as producing a set of accounts, servicing a car, or making a widget. They would not be responsible for the design of the task or planning the resources required in order to complete it.

Typical tasks assigned at an operational level include contributing to the output of a product or service, such as by checking the quality of finished products coming off a conveyor belt, helping to box the product or to deliver it.

A number of comparisons can be made between the layers in the organisation, as shown in Figure 20 on the next page.

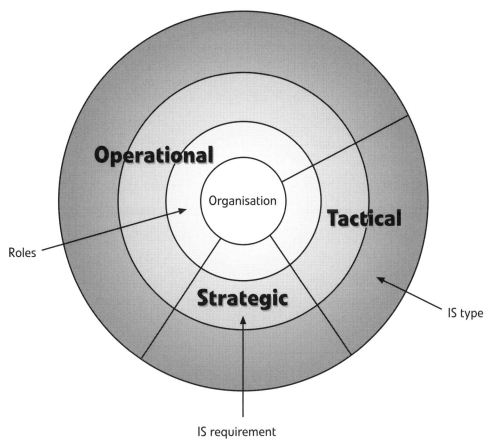

Figure 20

Levels and needs of personnel within an organisation

Information system requirements

The information system requirements and the types of system that would be used by different levels of personnel are shown in the table below. To an extent, these are interchangeable at strategic and tactical levels.

Level	Roles	Requirement	Type
Strategic	Senior management	Leading, directing, representing	Executive information system Decision-support system Management information system
Tactical or implementation	Middle management	Directing, representing, supervising, supporting, advising	Decision-support system Management information system Expert system Knowledge-based system
Operational	Productive workforce	Processing, practising, doing	Transaction-processing system Office automation system Process control system Data-processing system

Test your knowledge

1 Identify three layers of personnel within an organisation, and provide a list of possible roles and tasks that they would undertake.

2 What type of personnel would undertake the following tasks?

- decide on mergers and take-overs
- make widgets on a production line
- hire and fire staff
- plan a sales promotion
- work on a check-out desk
- attend strategy meetings.

3 What type of information systems would be needed for:
- senior managers
- middle managers
- production levels?

 Activity 7

Interview six people you know who work for an organisation. Try to vary the sample to get a mixture of age and experience.

1 Ask each person a set of questions to determine the following:
- their job role
- the tasks they do in a typical day/week
- the level (operational, tactical or strategic) they think they work at.

2 Produce a table comparing the answers of the six people interviewed.

3 Do the job roles and tasks described by each fit the characteristics of the three levels (operational, tactical and strategic)?

 Exam questions

1 The owner of an independent driving school, which employs six instructors, decides to get a local software house to write a bespoke package to manage client information, including the booking of lessons, the tracking of progress, and the recording of payments.

(a) Identify **two** different potential users of this system.   *(2 marks)*
(b) With the aid of examples, describe the different levels of information that each of these two users might require.   *(6 marks)*

AQA Jan 2003

2 Describe, with the aid of an example, the meaning of formal information flow within an organisation.   *(3 marks)*

AQA June 2002

4 Information and data

4.0 Data

Data is a set of random, unprocessed facts that has little or no value until it has undergone some kind of processing. The processing activity converts the data into information. The random, unprocessed characteristic of data can mean that prior to processing it may need to be sorted or translated, before it can be input into a system. The way in which this is done will depend upon the data capture tool.

There are a number of ways in which data can be captured and input into systems. Some of the most common methods include:

- keyboards
- bar-code readers
- optical devices
- swipe cards.

Each of these methods has a number of benefits and drawbacks in terms of accurate data entry.

The quantity and quality of data will influence the choice of data capture method and the accuracy of the input process. An operator typing in pages and pages of data using a keyboard will inevitably produce more errors than someone who scans the information in. However, using a keyboard gives an operator the ability to input unprocessed and raw data. With

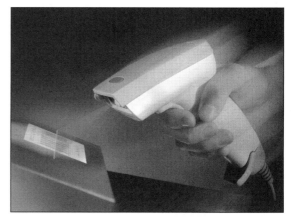

One way that data can be captured is through a bar-code reader

a reader or optical device, data has to be in a predetermined format for successful input.

A number of control mechanisms can be used to ensure the quality of input data. These mechanisms allow for checks in accuracy and completeness when data is entered into a system. There are a number of specific input controls for:

- authorisation
- data conversion
- data editing
- error handling.

Input data must be properly **authorised**, recorded and monitored as source documents flow to the system. For example, controls can be set up to authorise only selected personnel from the accounts department to produce budgets and forecasts for an MIS.

Input data must be properly **converted**, with few or no errors, as it is transcribed from one form to another, or between systems. Transcription errors can be reduced by keying input data directly onto the system or by using some form of automation.

Edit controls include various programmed routines that can edit data for errors before it is processed. Data that does not meet edit criteria can be rejected. Edit routines can produce a list of **errors** to be corrected at a later date, as shown in the table on the next page.

Reasonableness checks	Data must fall within certain boundaries set in advance, or it will be rejected
Format checks	Characteristics of the data, such as letter or digit length, are checked
Existence checks	Input data is compared to tables or master files to make sure that only valid codes are being used
Dependency checks	Checks are made to see whether a logical relationship is maintained between data for the same transaction or process

Test your knowledge

1. Identify with examples three ways in which data can be captured.
2. What sort of data is captured when a loyalty card is used?
3. How can the quantity and quality of data impact upon the data capture method?
4. What control mechanisms can be used to guarantee the quality of input data?

4.1 Information

Managers need information on a day-to-day basis. They perform a number of functions, including:

- making decisions
- delegating tasks
- motivating, leading and supporting staff
- generating reports.

In order to carry out these functions effectively, they need access to quality information that is relevant, up-to-date, specific and task driven.

Information can be characterised in a number of different ways that reflect its overall quality. The attributes of information can be divided into three different categories:

- time
- content
- form.

Time	Content	Form	Additional characteristics
Timeliness	Accuracy	Clarity	Confidence in source
Currency	Relevance	Detail	Reliability
Frequency	Completeness	Order	Received by correct person
Time period	Conciseness	Presentation	Sent by correct channels
	Scope	Media	

Time

The **time** category describes the time or frequency at which it is received. Information should be available when needed (timeliness). It should reflect the current environment and be adaptable for changes in the future (currency).

Access to information may be needed at regular intervals – every minute, hour, day or week (frequency). Quality information also covers the correct period of time, for example when checking last year's sales (time period).

Content

The **content** category examines the correctness of the information (accuracy), how applicable the information is to a given situation (relevance) and how comprehensive the information is (completeness). The information should be supplied in an efficient format, for example graphs or charts to show large quantities of numeric information (conciseness). Finally, information should be appropriate and meaningful to the recipient (scope).

Form

The **form** category ensures that the information is presented in a clear and appropriate format for the recipient (clarity) and that it is at the correct level and depth (detail).

Other quality factors in this category examine the ordering of the information (order), how the information is presented (presentation), and the appropriateness of the tool of transmission (media), for example sales figures should be communicated in a report, not an e-mail.

Other characteristics

A number of additional characteristics can be used to assess the quality of information, including confidence in the source of the information and issues of reliability.

Other more generic characteristics of information include the following.

1 **Source** – internal, external, primary, secondary. The source of information is important because it raises questions about how reliable the information is. If the information has been passed down through a number of channels (secondary information), how accurate is it? Internal and external information will affect the day-to-day operations of a business differently, as discussed on pages 45–47.

2 **Nature** – quantitative, qualitative, formal, informal. The nature of the information will affect how it is presented, interpreted and passed on.

   Quantitative information is based on facts and statistics, and is vital for planning, forecasting and decision-making. Examples of this type of information include monthly expenditure, sales figures or employee performance status. Quantitative information is essential when working with large data sets because facts and figures are easier to map and model as opposed to descriptive, qualitative information. **Qualitative** information provides the details. For example, you might know that a customer shops weekly but the qualitative aspect will identify preferences about certain products. One of the best ways to extract qualitative information is through interviewing, which allows you to obtain information that can serve as a balance to pure facts and figures.

3 **Level** – strategic, tactical, operational. Within an organisation there are three distinct levels, and information requirements at each level will be different.

For example, in a supermarket, **strategic** information would be needed for plans to open or close branches, introduce or scrap product lines, or invest more money into certain areas such as the bakery. **Tactical** information would be needed for decisions about increasing or reducing staffing levels, changing job roles, training and development, which product items to stock over a certain period and in what quantity, and so on. **Operational** information would be needed to ensure that shelves are stocked, stock is re-ordered, shelf life is checked, items are priced and positioned correctly, and so on.

4 **Time** – historical, current, future. Time characteristics allow users to identify when information was generated and communicated, and how significant that information is to the current environment. Some information is irrelevant because it is too outdated, for example the price of a computer last year. However, historical data can be useful, especially if an organisation is looking back to identify trends over a certain period in order to make predictions about the future.

5 **Frequency** – real-time, hourly, daily, monthly. The frequency of information is very important within an IT environment, especially when information systems are being used. The frequency at which information is input into a system, processed and output must be correctly designed to save an organisation time and money. For example, up-to-date information about customer buying patterns is vital.

6 **Use** – planning, control, decision-making. Information can be used for many different purposes in an organisation, including planning, processing, forecasting, decision-making, controlling and supporting.

An information system can help managers to carry out these functions more efficiently, cost effectively and productively.

7 **Form** – written, visual, aural, sensory. Information can take on a number of different formats, including verbal, written, visual and expressive, as shown in the table below.

Verbal	Written	Visual	Expressive
Directing	Letters	Charts	Using sign language
Advising	Memos	Maps	Pointing
Informing	Minutes	Graphs	Smiling
Challenging	Reports	Photographs	Frowning
Debating	Agendas	Designs	Laughing
Persuading	Invoices	Moving images	Crying
Delegating	Statements	Drawings	Hugging
Enquiring	Receipts	Static images	Waving

In the course of a day any number of these ways of communicating information may be used.

8 **Type** – disaggregated, aggregated, random. The way in which information is presented in terms of its structure and type can depend on the initial data source. For example, information about how many consumers buy a certain product could be based on survey information gathered from a sample of customers.

What does this mean?	
Aggregated information:	Information that has been collected and grouped or combined together in a meaningful way.
Disaggregated information:	Information that has been separated into its component parts.
Random information:	Information that has been collected together with no defined order or collective structure.

Test your knowledge

1 What are the three categories of attributes which information has?
2 Identify and describe four generic characteristics of information.
3 What is the difference between qualitative and quantitative information?
4 Give examples of information requirements at the following levels:
   ▪ strategic
   ▪ tactical
   ▪ operational.
5 How can information be used within an organisation?

Activity 8

Copy the following table and complete it by giving an example of how the piece of information could be used within an organisation, and by whom.

Information requirement	Example of use	By whom
Planning		
Processing		
Forecasting		
Decision-making		
Controlling		
Supporting and guiding		

Internal and external information requirements

The information requirements of an organisation can be broken down into internal information and external information.

Internal information can come from the following sources:

▪ employees
▪ functional departments (such as sales, IT, human resources, marketing, finance or operations).

The type of information that is generated or captured by these departments is shown below.

- **Sales** How many product or service types have been sold; how quickly these product or service types sold; pricing strategies; the feasibility of launching a new product or service; whether to diversify into new markets or ranges
- **IT** Issues connected with computer systems – crashes, down-times, or new systems on-line; number of users on the system; security; IT strategies – designing a company website, investing in upgrades, or networking issues
- **HR** Training strategies; hiring and firing; disciplinary actions; internal policies and procedures such as health and safety, code of practice, or equal opportunities
- **Marketing** Which product/service to promote; when to promote; how much to promote; where to promote and in what format
- **Finance** Profit, loss and budgeting; money to invest or for diversifying; deficit and growth areas; salaries and pensions
- **Operations** How many products have been produced; productivity levels; raw materials and cost of production; stock levels; delivery and despatch issues.

External information comes from outside the boundaries of an organisation. Sources of external information can be seen in Figure 21.

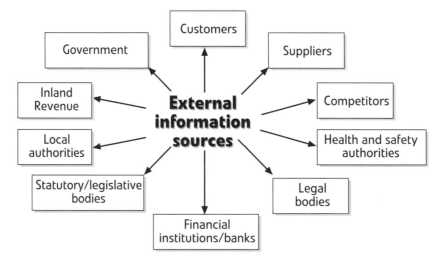

Figure 21

External information sources

Information from these sources will influence the way in which an organisation functions. For example, three of the more common external sources of information for a supermarket are shown in the table below.

Information captured from	Information requirement	Impact
Customers	What customers buy When customers buy How much they buy How much they spend Where they buy it	Alter stock levels to meet demands. Design promotional offers to tempt customers to buy more of a product or similar products. Move the position of certain stock items. Send out coupons and money-off vouchers for certain products.

Information captured from	Information requirement	Impact
Suppliers	How much they can supply When they can supply it (seasonally) How fast they can deliver it How much it will cost Reliability Quality of product	Offer certain stock items only at certain times – e.g. new potatoes only in the spring/summer months. Allow prices to fluctuate in line with supply and demand. Use additional suppliers to ensure delivery or quality or to cut costs.
Competitors	Market share Current offers and promotions Pricing policies Items stocked	Cut costs, improve operations, reduce overheads, offer more products, and expand the business. Increase promotional activity. Carry out market research to find out what customers want. Increase or decrease prices. Stock more or fewer products.

 Test your knowledge

1. Why do organisations need both internal and external information?
2. Give five examples of internal information.
3. Where can internal knowledge be derived from?
4. Identify four sources of external information and analyse the type of information each would provide to an organisation.

 Activity 9

Copy the table below and complete it, identifying the information requirements for each different organisation.

Organisation type	External information source	Information requirement
Car servicing depot	Customer	
	Parts supplier	
Hospital	Patient	
	Local authority/government	
School/college	Student	
	Funding bodies	
Builder's merchant	Health and safety authorities	
	Competitors	

Quality information

Figure 22 shows some of the factors that influence the quality of information.

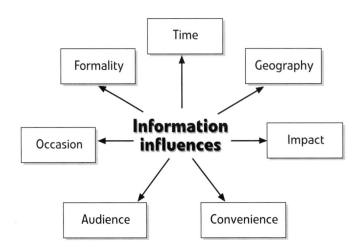

Figure 22

Factors affecting the quality of information

- **Time** The means of communicating information may be chosen according to the time it would take to transmit it. For example, it might be necessary to send a document by fax rather than post because of the urgency with which the information is needed.
- **Geography** The distance over which information has to travel will also influence the way in which it is transmitted. Telephone or e-mail may be the best way to send information over a distance of say ten miles.
- **Impact** The impression that you need to create will influence the way in which you communicate information. You would not bid for a million-pound deal by sending an e-mail; you might deliver a presentation in person, and send written confirmation of terms. A contact of employment would not be sent as an e-mail; it would be set out in a formal letter.
- **Convenience** Some methods of sharing information are more convenient than others. Writing a letter can be quite time consuming if there is a lot to say, and a telephone conversation may be more appropriate if there are points you need to confirm with the recipient.
- **Audience** The audience for the information will influence the way in which it is communicated. Within an organisation you might speak informally to a colleague, e-mail a team leader and send a memorandum to all the members of the department.
- **Occasion** The occasion can determine the way in which information is communicated; for example, you might send a card for a birthday.
- **Formality** There are some instances where information needs to be communicated in a specific way to match the formality of the situation. Written information is needed to make certain contracts and transactions legally binding. Birth, marriage and death certificates, employment contracts, guarantees and receipts are all in the form of standard documents.

The use of applications software can also affect the quality of information. If the application tool used is appropriate – such as using presentation software to deliver a talk on current sales figures – then it can enhance the process of communicating information. Effective use of applications is essential in an organisation where the majority of information exchange is completed electronically.

Factors that should be taken into consideration in terms of delivering good information include:

- relevance of the information to the recipient
- accuracy of the information, and whether the source is reliable
- completeness – does the information cover all the recipient's requirements?
- clarity – is the information presented at the right level of detail, and understandable?
- the confidence of the sender and recipient
- reaching the right person at the right time and in the right format.

4.2 Effective presentation

Good presentation skills are essential at work, as people will expect you to be able to present information in a clear, concise and relevant way.

The method and style of presenting a message can have a strong impact upon the recipient of that message. Some messages can be delivered in a written format such as a report, newsletter or formal letter. Others could be delivered in a more visual format through the use of charts, graphs and pictures.

The use of presentation tools and software can enhance oral delivery of information. An oral presentation can be delivered:

- formally or informally
- using ICT resources or with no ICT resource use
- to a wide audience, or to individuals.

Formal presentations can include:

- providing feedback on a project
- presenting information at a meeting
- announcing a press release
- giving a speech at an awards ceremony.

Informal presentations can include:

- a presentation given as part of your coursework
- telling a friend about your holiday
- giving a thank you or congratulations speech to friends or family.

The formality of a presentation will differ depending upon the environment in which it is being delivered and the intended audience. Formal presentations tend to be more structured and take more time in planning and delivery. They may be delivered to an audience that is not known to you, especially in an organisational environment.

Presentations can be formal or informal

In informal presentations you are more likely to be talking 'ad lib', with little or no preparation. Informal presentations often encourage spontaneous speech.

Some people find it difficult to recall large amounts of information and therefore need a prompt to aid them when speaking, such as small index cards containing a few bullet points.

Presentations can be delivered by:

- speaking spontaneously, or with the aid of cards or notes
- using presentation software
- using aids such as flip charts, overhead transparencies (OHTs), a whiteboard, etc.

Although these presentation aids do help you to communicate information, they can also be quite restrictive in terms of the delivery. When you are delivering a presentation using cards or notes, remember the following.

- The information on cards or in notes should be kept to a minimum, using bullet points only.
- You should only glance at the aids, not read from them.
- Ideally, you should place these aids on a desk or podium. If you need to hold them, ensure that they are not held high, obscuring your face.
- Maintain a rapport with the audience by establishing eye contact and acknowledging their responses with a smile or a nod.
- Use your voice to be in control of the presentation and capture the audience's attention. The problem with reading information out is that sometimes your tone and expression are lost, and your voice is pitched at a monotonous level.
- Do not rush through each bullet point – use your creativity to expand on the information.

Presentations without notes or other aids are usually given by people who:

- know their topic inside out
- feel enthusiastic about and motivated by the topic, and can therefore rely on body language to demonstrate this
- feel comfortable with their target audience
- draw heavily on the responses and participation of the audience.

ICT has played a big role in changing the way in which presentations are delivered and the overall quality of presentations. Presentation software can provide a number of benefits, as shown in Figure 23.

Figure 23

Benefits of using presentation software

Presentation software can provide a range of features that will enable you to:

- customise slide backgrounds
- control the speed of each slide

- determine the way in which the slide appears on the screen (dissolving in, for example)
- automatically time the length of each slide
- link to other applications or the Internet.

Other aids such as flip charts, whiteboards or OHTs can assist you in the delivery of a presentation. Flip charts are often used in business presentations to show sales figures, forecast charts and projection graphs.

Flip charts are also useful if you want to encourage audience participation, as ideas can be noted down and discussed. OHTs are commonly used to display facts and figures and in some cases are preferable to using cards or notes.

Test your knowledge

1 Give two examples each of formal and informal presentations.
2 What are the benefits of using ICT to deliver a presentation?
3 How can you customise a presentation using presentation software?
4 Identify three aids that you can use to help you deliver a presentation. What are the benefits of each?

Activity 10

Prepare two 10-minute presentations.

Presentation 1

For this presentation you can choose your own topic area. Some suggestions include:

- a hobby or pastime
- a holiday
- a special occasion
- sports
- pop music
- films or TV.

This presentation should last 10 minutes and must be delivered without presentation resources. However, you can bring in items to show as part of your presentation.

Presentation 2

You have applied for a job in a large IT company. You have been successful in the first round of interviews and have now been asked to attend a second round to assess your ability to communicate to a group.

Prepare a 10-minute presentation based on one of the following topic areas:

- the need for team working
- the need to communicate at all levels in an organisation
- the need to delegate
- the need to problem solve.

You have half an hour in which to prepare a presentation using any resources available. Deliver the presentation to your group.

Write a short report evaluating and comparing the two presentations in terms of their ease of preparation and effectiveness in communicating information. Ask for feedback on them.

Exam questions

1 Puregreens, a retailer of organic vegetables, has recently launched a marketing website. The e-mail response from the 'contact us' button has been overwhelming, so they are thinking of expanding into selling on-line.

Discuss the implications of this, paying particular attention to the following:

- methods of data capture that will be available for on-line or off-line payment
- the control and audit issues associated with this method of selling
- the information needs of the management of this system
- the additional information that might be generated.

(20 marks)

AQA Jan 2003

2 A company keeps records of its sales and uses a Management Information System to produce reports for its sales personnel, and for its shareholders.

(a) Describe **two** differences between the information needed by sales personnel in their day-to-day work, and by shareholders reading the annual report. *(4 marks)*

(b) Describe, with the aid of an example, **one** characteristic of good quality information that might be produced by this system. *(3 marks)*

AQA June 2002

3 Describe **four** characteristics of good information. *(8 marks)*

AQA June 2003

5 The management of change

The introduction of an information system can evoke many changes in an organisation. Some of these changes may be welcomed by employees because they enhance or support individual job tasks or roles. Other changes may be met with opposition if they are seen as a threat to individual job tasks or roles.

In order to maintain a balance and prevent any negative reactions to the introduction or development of an information system, careful planning, implementation and management need to be in place.

5.0 Areas of change

Issues that might need to be addressed are shown in Figure 24.

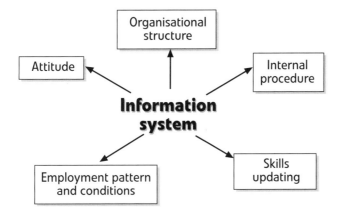

Figure 24

Areas of change resulting from the introduction of an information system

Organisational structure

The structure of an organisation may change as a result of introducing an information system. If procedures become more efficient and productivity increases with less human input needed, a restructuring may occur with possible job losses. This de-layering may take out some middle management roles, flattening the structure, as discussed on page 8.

Internal procedures

Internal procedures and processing activities within an organisation can change, especially at an operational level where repetitive tasks are automated. An information system at a tactical level may help with decisions about how operations function, and changes to procedures may be made after identifying weaknesses in the existing system.

Skills updating

The introduction of an information system could result in employers having to update their employees' skills and knowledge, especially if the new information system will play a role in their job tasks. Extensive re-training may be appropriate for staff at all levels.

Employment pattern and conditions

Job roles and tasks may change as a result of the introduction of an information system. If the system has been implemented to carry out tasks of a repetitive nature this would release some employees for more complex tasks. Automating some tasks may result in longer hours, different shift patterns or even relocation for staff involved with the new system.

Attitude

Some employees and employers are reluctant to embrace change, and the introduction of an information system could generate a number of feelings ranging from doubt to anxiety. Unless all staff are kept up to date with developments, the culture and attitude of individuals within an organisation could worsen, with resentment developing between employees and employers.

5.1 Steps to success

To address some of these challenges and ensure that the introduction of an information system is successful, a number of steps can be taken.

Step 1: Inform end users

The new information system will be used to support employees at a particular level, and this message should be shared with those concerned so that they do not see it as a threat. Issues of ownership will disperse if all users are kept well informed.

Step 2: Integrate systems

The new information system should be well integrated with existing systems. Failure to do so will mean potential disruptions to the smooth running of the organisation.

Step 3: Plan the implementation

Implementation of the information system should be carefully planned to ensure that there are minimal disruptions to end users and to day-to-day operations.

Step 4: Support the system

Training and development may be required so that end users know how to use the new information system. Any training requirements should be identified before installing the information system.

Test your knowledge

1   Give reasons why the introduction of an information system in an organisation may cause negative feelings among employees.
2   Why might an organisation have to invest in more up-to-date technology if an information system is being introduced?
3   Identify four changes that might occur as a result of the introduction of an information system.
4   How might these changes be dealt with?

Exam question

1   The introduction of an information system is likely to result in changes to an organisation. State **three** factors that will need to be managed to ensure a smooth period of change.

(3 marks)

AQA June 2003

2   New information and communication technologies are frequently introduced into companies as a result of outdated existing systems, market pressure, new legislation and other factors. Companies have to adapt quickly, or face going out of business.

Discuss the factors that need to be considered to manage such changes successfully within an organisation. Particular attention should be given to:

▨   organisation structure and information needs

▨   management and staffing issues

▨   internal procedures, external procedures and the customer interface.

Illustrate your answer with specific examples.   *(20 marks)*

The quality of written communication will be assessed in your answer.

AQA June 2002

6 **Legal aspects**

6.0 Corporate IS security policies

Computer systems and information systems are critical to organisations, offering support to all levels of management. The value placed on this level of support is so great that failure of a system for even a short period could paralyse an organisation and cost it thousands if not hundreds of thousands of pounds.

Many organisations invest large amounts of money in the development and implementation of a security policy. This policy will be designed to minimise errors, disasters, computer crime and breaches of security by outlining control mechanisms and the sanctions and penalties enforceable in the case of a breach of security or a crime being committed.

The idea behind a security policy is to make all employees aware of the procedures that have been put in place and their role in contributing to the safety of systems.

Corporate information system security policies are based on a number of criteria, such as:

- prevention of misuse
- detection of misuse or errors
- investigation of misuse or errors
- procedures for security
- staff responsibilities
- disciplinary procedures.

Control mechanisms can be used in the prevention of misuse. These can be broken down into two areas:

- general controls
- application controls.

General controls

General controls ensure the effective operation of procedures in all application areas. These include the following:

- Implementation controls. The systems development process is audited at various stages to ensure that the process is properly controlled and managed. The audit should examine the level of user involvement, costs and quality assurance techniques at each stage of implementation.

- Hardware controls. These ensure that the system is physically secure and that no system malfunctions have occurred. Hardware controls can include restricting access to only authorised personnel; protection against fire, extreme humidity and temperature fluctuations; back-ups and power failure plans; parity checks to detect system malfunctions; validity checks; echo checks – verifying that hardware devices are performance-ready.

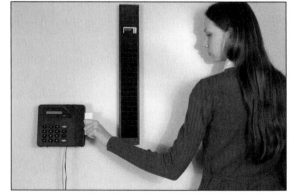

Hardware controls include ensuring that access is restricted to only authorised personnel

- Software controls. The use of systems software is monitored to prevent unauthorised access to software programs, systems software and computer programs.
- Data security controls. These ensure that valuable data files are not subject to unauthorised access, change or destruction. Control mechanisms are required for data files when they are in use and held in storage. On-line data must also be protected against unauthorised personnel.
- Computer operations controls. Checks must be carried out to ensure that programmed procedures are consistently and correctly applied to the storage and processing of data. These would usually be carried out by the IT department. The controls would cover the set-up of processing jobs, operations software, computer operations and back-up and recovery procedures.
- Administrative, standards and procedural controls. Administrative controls are formalised standards, procedures and control disciplines to ensure that the organisation's general and application controls are properly executed and enforced. The most important administrative controls are written policies and procedures, supervision practices and segregation of functions.

Written policies and procedures establish formal standards for controlling information system operations. These policies should be available to all employees and be addressed through training and development sessions aimed at creating awareness of the organisation's security policy.

Staff should take responsibility for identifying the measures and controls in place. Correct supervision of personnel involved in control procedures ensures that the controls are performing as intended. Without supervision, the best-designed set of controls may be by-passed, or neglected.

Staff who do not support the corporate information system security policy or who neglect to carry out the procedures set down in the policy may face disciplinary action, ranging from a formal warning to suspension or dismissal.

Application controls

Application controls are specific controls within each separate computer application, such as accounts or stock control. They include automated and manual procedures that ensure only authorised data is processed by that application.

Application controls can be broken down into three areas:

- input controls
- processing controls
- output controls.

Input controls check data for accuracy and completeness when entered into the system, using validation processes.

Processing controls establish that data is complete and accurate during updating. The major processing controls are:

- run control totals – reconciling input control totals with the totals of items that have updated the file
- computer matching – matching the input data with information held on master or suspense files.

Output controls ensure that the results of computer processing are accurate, complete and properly distributed. Typical output controls include:

- balancing output totals with input processing totals
- reviewing computer processing logs to determine whether all computer tasks have been executed properly
- time and date stamps on printed or electronic output or use of version numbers, to ensure that the correct output is distributed
- formal procedures and documentation specifying authorised recipients of output reports, checks or other documents.

Content of a security policy

The contents of a corporate IS security policy will vary between organisations, but there are some common features that will form the basis of a policy. These include:

- access controls – identifying and authenticating users within the system, setting up passwords, building in detection tools, encrypting sensitive data
- administrative controls – setting up procedures with personnel in case of a breach, disciplinary actions, defining standards and screening of personnel at the time of hiring
- operations controls – back-up procedures and controlling access through smart cards, log-in and log-out procedures and other control tools
- personnel controls – creating a general awareness among employees, providing training and education
- physical controls – securing and locking hardware, having a back-up facility off-site, etc.

Improving awareness

In order to create more awareness throughout the organisation, a number of steps can be taken to increase the profile of the IS security policy. These include:

1 Ensuring that all new staff members have been briefed about the IS security policy.

2 Updating existing staff members regularly on security policy content.

3 Providing training opportunities and development sessions to encourage good IT working practices.

4 Making staff members aware of the implications for them of not enforcing the security policy.

5 Taking any action required in order to ensure that the security policy is adhered to.

Test your knowledge

1 What are the two types of control mechanisms?
2 Identify four aspects of hardware controls.
3 Why is there a need to have written policies and procedures in regard to IS security?
4 What are the three elements of application controls?

6.1 Audit requirements

Auditing allows an organisation to take stock at a point in time.

Software auditing provides an opportunity to check that what is on the system has been authorised and is legal. Over a period of time a number of factors could impact upon how much software an organisation acquires without its knowledge. These can include:

- illegal copying of software by employees
- downloading of software by employees
- installation of software by employees
- use of software exceeding licence.

These interventions by employees may occur with little or no consideration of the organisation's responsibility to ensure that software is not misused.

Audits can also be carried out to identify and correct data. A **data quality audit** is a structured survey of the accuracy and level of completeness of data in an information system. This type of audit can be carried out using the following methods:

- surveying end users to gather their perceptions on data quality
- surveying samples gathered from data files
- surveying entire data files.

Unless regular data quality audits are undertaken, organisations have no way of knowing to what extent their information systems contain inaccurate, incomplete or ambiguous information.

Audit trails can have a number of functions, such as checking to see what information has been added, changed or updated, when and by whom. Audit trails are written into applications and recorded as each transaction occurs, usually writing a record to an audit file.

The complexity of individual systems such as stock control, ordering or payroll and the networking of data could mean that an error in one data set is distributed among other systems. This could cause major problems that may lie undiscovered for days, weeks, months or even years.

Test your knowledge

1 Why do organisations need to carry out audits on software and data?
2 What could an audit uncover?
3 What factors could impact upon how much software an organisation acquires without its knowledge?
4 What is a data quality audit, and how can it be carried out?

6.2 Disaster recovery management

There are a number of threats to information systems. These include threats to:

- physical security
- personnel security
- communication security
- document security
- hardware security
- software security.

These threats can be assessed using risk analysis (see the next page). There can be a physical security threat to an information system where there is a risk of people stealing equipment or tampering with the data in the system. To overcome this, all hardware and software should be protected by locks (to the system and the room or storage environment), brackets and possibly CCTV or other monitoring systems.

Keeping electronic documents and data secure can be difficult because of the environment in which users work, the various levels of users within an organisation and the need to access documents or data stored on a system.

With the movement towards a totally networked environment promoting a culture of 'sharing', the issue of document and data security is even more important.

Data can be protected by introducing good practice measures such as backing up all data to a secondary storage device. The security of personal data is also a requirement under the Data Protection Act 1984.

Risk analysis

Risk analysis examines how liable an organisation is to security breaches based on its current security provisions.

Hackers are becoming more and more sophisticated in the tools and techniques that they use to gain unauthorised access to corporate systems, costing organisations thousands if not hundreds of thousands of pounds. Even the most advanced systems such as Visa are not infallible.

Case study – Fraudsters hit Visa for second time

by Danielle Rossingh

The credit card details of 'a large number' of Visa customers in America and Europe have been stolen from a US-based retailer, Visa said yesterday.

It is the second time this year that the credit card giant has fallen victim to an attempt to illegally obtain card numbers. Last February, a computer hacker gained access to 5 million Visa and MasterCard accounts in the US.

Visa yesterday said it was co-operating with the American authorities on the matter. It also said it had issued a fraud alert to its member banks after it was informed of an 'internal security breach' at the American retailer's database.

Although Visa declined to comment on the exact number of cards compromised because of the investigation, a spokesman for Visa Europe said: 'Everyone who used a credit card at this

© Telegraph Group Limited (2003)   *Telegraph* 11 June 2003

Further research

1. What steps can an organisation take to stop hackers gaining unauthorised access to their systems?
2. What penalties are enforceable against hackers?
3. What legislation has been set up to protect organisations against hackers?

Risk analysis involves:

- identifying the elements of an information system
- assessing the value of each element to the business
- identifying any threats to that element
- assessing the likelihood of that threat occurring.

Often, this is done as a mathematical exercise. The value of each element is multiplied by the risk factor for that element, giving a measure of overall risk. Guidelines will then tell the business how high a risk it is running so it can plan the defence of systems adequately.

Threats that can occur can be broken down into a number of areas, including:

- physical – theft of hardware, software or data
- personnel – staff deleting or overwriting data
- hardware – system crashes or processor meltdown
- confidentiality – hackers or espionage
- virus or Trojan – software damage caused maliciously
- natural – disasters such as fire, flood, earthquake or lightning
- electrical surge or power loss – overloading or disabling the system
- erroneous data – inaccurate data in the system.

Once potential threats and risks have been identified, policies can be put in place to address them. A corporate information systems security policy can be drawn up to address such threats, as discussed in Section 6.0 above.

Contingency plans

Contingency plans can be used to combat potential and actual threats to a system. Most organisations have a security policy that is open to continuous review and updating.

The structure of a contingency plan would be unique to an organisation and its requirements. Some organisations are more at risk than others, depending on:

- size
- proximity to areas prone to natural disasters such as floods
- location
- core business activity.

A contingency plan includes a back-up strategy for all data held and methods for recovering that data to get systems up and running in the event of a disaster.

A number of companies have been set up to provide 'disaster recovery' services. These companies will maintain copies of important data and files on behalf of an organisation.

Large organisations have many choices for contingency planning, including;

- subscribing to a disaster recovery service
- an arrangement with a company that runs compatible computer systems
- a secondary back-up site that is geographically distanced from the main site.

Smaller organisations might employ other measures such as a drive array or RAID system, or data warehousing facilities for backing up their systems. They will need to arrange recovery facilities in line with their budgets and operational requirements.

Test your knowledge

1. What are the broad categories of threats to information systems?
2. What security measures can be enforced within an organisation?
3. What is meant by the term *risk analysis*?
4. Why are some organisations more at risk than others in terms of potential threats to their systems?
5. What measures can a large and a small company take to protect their data?
6. What strategies exist to protect information systems from possible threats?

6.3 Legislation

A range of legislation aims to protect organisations, users of information systems and the general public about whom information may be stored.

The enforcement of this legislation can impact upon the procedures of organisations in a number of ways. In order to comply, an organisation will have to ensure that it operates within certain boundaries, including informing employees and third parties about how it intends to safeguard systems and any information collected, processed, copied, stored and output on these systems.

An organisation needs to consider how legislation affects everyday operations in terms of:

- collecting, processing and storing data
- using software
- protecting employees and ensuring that working conditions are of an acceptable standard.

Data Protection Act 1984 and 1988

The Data Protection Act applies to the processing of data and information about individuals. It places obligations on organisations and people who collect, process and store personal data about customers. The act is based on a set of principles that bind a user to maintain procedures for keeping data secure. The main principles include the following.

- Personal data should be processed fairly and lawfully.
- Personal data should be held only for one or more specified and lawful purposes.
- Personal data held should not be disclosed in any way incompatible with the specified and lawful purpose.
- Personal data held should be adequate and relevant, not excessive for the purpose or purposes.
- Personal data should be accurate and up to date.
- Personal data should not be retained for any longer than necessary.
- Individuals should be informed about personal data stored and should be entitled to have access to it, and if appropriate have such data corrected or erased.
- Security measures should ensure that no unauthorised access to, alteration, disclosure or destruction of personal data is permitted, and protect against accidental loss or destruction.

Computer Misuse Act 1990

The Computer Misuse Act addresses the threat of hackers trying to gain unauthorised access to computer systems. Before this act was passed there was little protection, and prosecutions were difficult because taking data by hacking was not considered to be deprivation to the owner (the definition of theft).

Copyright, Designs and Patent Act 1988

Software developers and organisations are protected against unauthorised copying of their software, designs, printed material and any other product by the Copyright, Designs and Patent Act. Under copyright legislation, organisations and developers can ensure that Intellectual Property Rights (IPR) have been safeguarded so that third parties cannot exploit their research and development.

Software piracy and misuse

Software piracy can be broken down into a number of key areas:

- recordable CD ROMs – pirates compile large amounts of software onto one recordable CD-ROM and make multiple copies
- professional counterfeits – copies of software are made including media, packages, licences and even security holograms, all to resemble the genuine article
- Internet piracy – the downloading or distribution of software via the Internet, infringing copyright
- corporate overuse – organisations install a software package onto more machines than they have licences for
- hard disk loaders – retail outlets or dealers load versions of software onto a computer system to encourage customers to buy their computer hardware. Customers will not have the appropriate licences or be entitled to other services such as technical support or upgrades.

Most organisations will have a policy about software use, as shown in the example in Figure 25. Software piracy and general misuse could result in severe penalties for both an employee and employer, as illustrated in Figure 26 on the next page.

SAMPLE
Corporate Software Policy

Corporate policy regarding the use of personal computer software.

1. **(Organization)** licenses the use of computer software from a variety of outside companies. **(Organization)** does not own this software or its related documentation, and unless authorized by the software developer, does not have the right to reproduce it except for back-up purposes.

2. **(Organization)** employees shall use the software only in accordance with the license agreements and will not install unauthorized copies of commercial software.

3. **(Organization)** employees shall not download or upload unauthorized software over the Internet.

4. **(Organization)** employees learning of any misuse of software or related documentation within the Company shall notify the department manager or **(Organization)**'s legal counsel.

5. According to applicable copyright law, persons involved in the illegal reproduction of software can be subject to civil damages and criminal penalties including fines and imprisonment. **(Organization)** does not condone the illegal duplication of software. **(Organization)** employees who make, acquire, or use unauthorized copies of computer software shall be disciplined as appropriate under the circumstances. Such discipline may include termination.

6. Any doubts concerning whether any employee may copy or use a given software program should be raised with a responsible manager.

I am fully aware of the software use policies of **(Organization)** and agree to uphold these policies.

Figure 25

Sample policy statement for software use

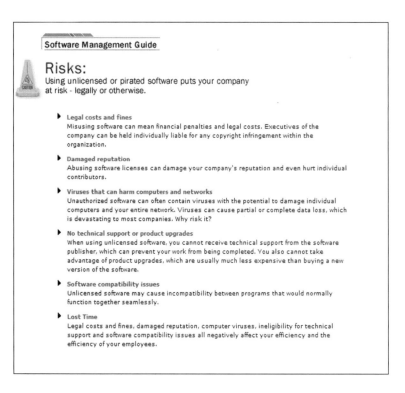

Figure 26

Guide to the risks of using unlicensed or pirated software

Health and safety

Organisations also have a responsibility to comply with health and safety measures. Consideration needs to be given to the working conditions of users, including the environmental, social and practical aspects. The only ICT-related aspect of this legislation is display screen equipment, although many of the ergonomic issues are also relevant to staff working with IT.

Enforcing and controlling legal responsibilities

A number of methods can be used to ensure compliance with data protection, software misuse, health and safety legislation. These are summarised in the table below.

Legislation	Methods of enforcing
Data protection	■ Employ a departmental data protection officer.
	■ Give detailed job descriptions to all employees.
	■ Have procedures in place to follow up any anomalies.
	■ Incorporate security measures such as the setting up of passwords, physical log-ins, firewalls and encryption.
	■ Have a strict code of practice for personal databases and software.
	■ Educate employees.
	■ Set out disciplinary procedures.
	■ Make use of access levels.
	■ Enforce network activity logging.

Legislation	Methods of enforcing
Software misuse	■ Do not permit employees to install unauthorised or unlicensed software.
	■ Do not permit employees to copy software for home or unlicensed use.
	■ Ensure that the organisation has a corporate hardware/software policy.
	■ Ensure that virus scanning takes place.
	■ Initiate regular audits.
	■ Institute disciplinary procedures.
Health and safety	■ Employ a health and safety officer.
	■ Regularly inspect work stations against health and safety and ergonomic criteria.
	■ Train staff in correct use of hardware and software, and legislation regarding health and safety issues.
	■ Set up procedures for ensuring that faulty equipment is replaced.
	■ Promote good health and safety practice.

Test your knowledge

1 Why will legislation have an impact on the procedures of an organisation?
2 Which legislation would an organisation need to adhere to if it was dependent on data processing and the use and support of information systems?
3 Why is it a good idea to have a policy on software use?
4 What are the risks of using pirated or unlicensed software?

Exam questions

1 A growing organisation has realised that so far they have been lucky in that their information systems have not failed. Before they expand their business operational reliance on ICT, they have been advised by their insurer to carry out a risk analysis and then plan what to do next.

(a) Explain what is meant by risk analysis. *(3 marks)*

(b) State **three** different potential threats to an information system, and describe a counter-measure for each one. *(9 marks)*

(c) Describe **three** of the criteria that could be used to select a disaster contingency plan. *(6 marks)*

AQA Jan 2003

2 Organisations that operate ICT systems have to comply with the relevant legislation. Most have procedures to ensure that this happens.

(a) Describe **three** methods of enforcing and controlling data protection legislation within an organisation. *(6 marks)*

(b) Describe **three** methods of enforcing and controlling software misuse legislation within an organisation. *(6 marks)*

(c) Describe **three** methods of enforcing and controlling health and safety legislation within an organisation. *(6 marks)*

AQA June 2003

7 User support

Organisations that rely on ICT will need help when problems occur. The levels of support available depend on a number of factors, as shown in Figure 27.

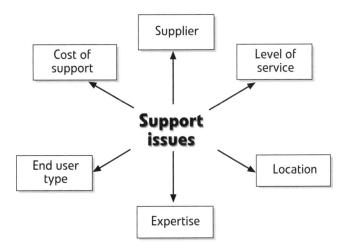

Figure 27

Support issues

- **Supplier** – the level of support offered depends on the source of the hardware or software; a large multinational supplier will probably offer a more comprehensive support infrastructure than a small independent provider.
- **Level of service** – higher levels of service and support may be offered to important end users depending on how much has been spent on products, hardware, software and existing support services.
- **Location** – this can have an impact on the level of support if a physical procedure such as a maintenance or repair has to be done; however, with today's technology, some support can be offered via the telephone, e-mail, Internet or through company bulletin boards.
- **Expertise** – support may be limited in certain technological areas due to the nature and specialism of the required support. Only larger software houses may be able to provide support because they will have the money to invest in training staff in the required areas.
- **End user type** – different end users require different levels of support. A home user may require remote support for software difficulties, whereas a networked business user may require specialist support in terms of setting up systems, routing or other system communication issues.
- **Cost of support** – this may have a direct impact on the level of support received. Some software houses may provide certain support free of charge based on a question-and-answer basis. Other, more hands-on support may be chargeable depending upon the requirement.

7.0 Supporting users

User support can be offered in a number of different ways, including the following.

- User groups – forums and user groups provide an interactive way of getting support on various issues relating to hardware, software and communications systems. People who may have experienced the same difficulties, or experts, will be on hand to answer any queries.

■ Bulletin boards – on-line advice may be offered via a posting on a bulletin board.

■ E-mail – advice may be offered directly through e-mail.

■ Articles and features – a growing number of magazines and journals are devoted to IT and to specific systems or software types. They often provide step-by-step guides or question-and-answer pages giving advice to users.

■ Documentation – user support can include instruction manuals and booklets, and user guides. For some users, the instruction manuals provided with products are informative.

■ Utilities – software houses can provide utilities to help users to diagnose and solve problems. Tools available include logging system activities to record problems, anti-virus software and disc fragmenters. However, new users may not fully understand the technical language or what is being asked of them when installing software or upgrading versions of existing software. Guides and manuals can be more user-friendly as they incorporate graphics and step-by-step instructions.

■ For specialised systems provided by a software house or package supplier, a technician may stay on site or visit.

Case study – Microsoft

Microsoft is one of the largest providers of systems software to a host of customers including home users, small business users, networked users and multinational organisations. The product range available is extensive, including:

■ operating system software
■ applications software
■ utility software
■ business and development software.

For each piece of software sold, Microsoft has to ensure that support is available in case there are any problems, such as:

■ installation difficulties
■ program difficulties
■ incompatibility issues
■ software conflicts
■ bugs and software errors.

Available support will be depend on a range of factors as shown in Figure 27 on page 67.

For products released onto the market, Microsoft has produced a 'product support life-cycle', identifying phases of support:

Years 1–5   Mainstream support

Years 6 and 7   Extended support

Years 8+   On-line self-help support (for business and development software only)

The levels of support available to Microsoft's customers include:

■ free support
■ personal support
■ professional support
■ premier support.

Except free support, each of these levels carries a charge payable per incident, or per incident pack, as shown in Figure 28 on the next page. Other system support services available to end users include:

■ downloadable software

■ patches

■ access to on-line help, weekly 'how to' information.

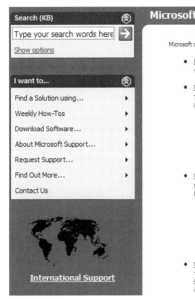

Figure 28

Levels of support

 Further research

Microsoft offers various levels of support to different types of user. Using Microsoft as an example, carry out the following research activities.

1 Identify two other software system supply companies that provide user support and compare all three on the following criteria:
- who the support is aimed at (home user or business, etc.)
- the length of the support contract
- cost of the support
- logistics – whether support is offered over the phone, via e-mail, on-site or off-site.

2 Based on these criteria, state which one of the three providers offers:
- best value for money
- better quality.

 Test your knowledge

1 The level of support received from software houses can be dependent upon a number of factors. Identify and justify four of these.

2 In what ways might support requirements differ between a home user and a networked business user?

3 What levels of support are available to Microsoft's customers?

4 In what ways can user support be offered?

Activity 11

Research two software houses and:

- identify their customer base
- identify the level(s) of support available
- find out whether levels of support vary between different users
- find out whether the support is free or charged for.

7.1 Training

Training is one of the many overhead costs associated with employing new staff and updating the skills and knowledge of existing staff. The need to train staff is seen by most employers as vital, the cost being far outweighed by the benefits.

The costs of training include:

- trainer fees
- course fees
- accommodation costs
- materials and training packs
- working time lost while an employee is attending training.

The benefits of training include:

- a skilled and up-to-date workforce
- a motivated workforce
- greater efficiency, more productivity and a more competitive organisation
- a more flexible workforce that can adapt to changes in job tasks and roles.

At an operational level, training is practical and includes:

- application software training
- inventory and stock control
- accounts and payroll
- health and safety.

The majority of training at this level might involve a number of employees being trained at the same time, possibly in-house to cut costs.

The vast majority of training in an organisation will focus on the software it has. Applications training is probably the most sought-after because of the generic skills required by users across a range of functional areas.

There are a number of recognised training methods that can be used to instruct users, especially for applications training. These are discussed below.

In-house training of a number of employees at the same time will cut costs

Instructor-led training

This type of training can be carried out in-house or outside the organisation. It is usually carried out by a professional who specialises in a particular area such as applications software, programming, Internet, web applications or hardware. The instructor will lead the event and teach users through the use of demonstrations, practical activities, and examples.

Hands-on training

This is mainly based on observation – watching somebody doing the task, or 'sitting next to Nellie', and then carrying out the task under the guidance of the person who was being observed. This type of training can also be referred to as 'on-the-job' training.

On-line training

This method of training is extremely popular because it can be carried out in some cases at any time. Users can log onto a particular site, download materials and work through examples and activities at their own pace. CD Roms are another form of computer-based training.

Self-teach off-line

This can be accomplished with user training manuals or videos. Individuals learn or update skills by reading materials and applying what they have learnt to a range of exercises or practical activities. This method of training is especially popular for ICT professional qualification status, in terms of becoming Microsoft or Cisco accredited. Sometimes these programmes of study are assessed on-line.

Training policies

The way in which training can be delivered will depend on an organisation's training strategy. Some organisations develop their own strategy for a specific time frame, for example over a period of six months or a year. This strategy may include:

- training type – hardware, software or specialist such as payroll or health and safety training
- personnel to be trained – all new employees, functional departments, supervisors
- delivery format – instructor-led, hands-on, self-teach, on-line
- location – in-house, residential, day release.

Another training strategy option would be to out-source to other companies, especially if the level of training required is quite specialist – see Figure 29 on the next page for an example.

Continual updating and refreshing of skills is beneficial for both employees and employers. For an employee, skills updating may give the opportunity to move into a new job role, or become more marketable. For an employer, a well-trained workforce could reduce costs and inefficiencies and make the company more competitive.

Services

Training Strategies offers you the opportunity to create your own training sessions based on your specific industry needs.

Every business is different but the application and approach to training is standard throughout all industries. Training Strategies has 20 years of experience in designing and developing many kinds of training using any delivery system from web-based training to self study.

Figure 29

Training Strategies offers to provide specialised training

 Test your knowledge

1 Identify three benefits of training.
2 What type of training would be typical of the following users?
   - managing director
   - supervisor
   - computer operator
   - payroll assistant
3 Identify three ways of training a system user. What do you feel are the benefits of each of the training methods you have selected?

 Activity 12

You work in the training department of a manufacturing company. You have been asked by human resources to produce a one-day training plan for a piece of applications software for up to 10 system users.

1 What type of information will you require before drawing up the plan?
2 Prepare a training plan to include the following information:
   - timetable for the day
   - list of aims and objective
   - list of practical activities and information sessions
   - timings for each activity/session.

Exam questions

1 Describe, with the aid of examples, **three** different methods of providing training in the use of software, and justify their use. *(9 marks)*

AQA Jan 2003

2 A small legal firm is about to replace stand-alone computers with a new computer network. Industry standard software will be installed. As new users of both the equipment and the software, the firm is concerned about the levels of support and training that will be needed. There are three levels of system user – the solicitors themselves, the practice management and the administrative staff.

(a) Explain **two** factors that need to be taken into account when planning the training.

(4 marks)

(b) Describe **two** different ways of giving technical support to these users.

(4 marks)

(c) State **two** means of providing the training material, and give an advantage of each.

(4 marks)

AQA June 2002

8 Project management and effective ICT teams

There are a number of factors to consider when taking on a project and working in a project environment. Depending on the scope and nature of the project, a number of people may be involved and tasks may be allocated to teams rather than individuals.

All projects follow a life-cycle that extends from the initial investigation through to the final evaluation. A traditional project life-cycle model can be seen in Figure 30.

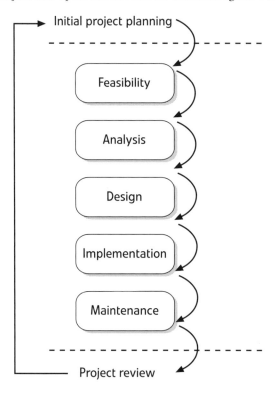

Figure 30

Project life-cycle model

The structure of a team can be broken down into three basic categories – the creative, tactical and problem-solving work. These can be analysed in conjunction with project life-cycle phases, as shown in the table below.

Category	Life-cycle phase	Characteristics of team
Creative	Designing	A high degree of autonomy is required in order to explore a range of options and possibilities. The team would require independent thinkers and self-starters.
Tactical	Doing	This calls for a very structured team, which can plan, set and clarify objectives for individual team members. It should be a motivated team that can work well together.
Problem-solving	Doing/ developing	This team needs to focus on the final resolution, overcoming problems as a team when they occur.

The size and composition of the team will depend on a number of factors, including:

- the budget of the project
- time constraints
- the complexity and level of the project
- the resources available.

Projects are often sub-divided into smaller tasks and activities that are delegated to individuals working in a project team. Disseminating the tasks in this way can ensure individuals are working on the areas they are considered to be experienced in and/or have received training for.

The characteristics of a good team include:

- strong leadership
- appropriate allocation of tasks
- ability to comply with standards
- systems for monitoring costs
- ways of controlling resources, activities and team members.

A team has to have some sort of coherence in order to function effectively. In order to maintain a certain level of efficiency a team needs to be directed by a team leader or project manager. This person will delegate tasks, manage the activities of the project, encourage team interaction and be accountable for the dynamics of the group.

When allocating tasks a team leader should look to the strengths of individuals. For example, if you are aware that a team member is good at designing websites he or she may be assigned tasks involving setting up and maintaining a website.

Ensuring that the team complies with standards is crucial to ensure that the project is carried out at the right level and within the agreed quality and procedural boundaries.

Managing costs is an essential part of any project, and failure to do so is the cause of many difficulties. Ensuring that the project team all work to schedule within agreed resources will mean that costs do not escalate. The control and monitoring of resources, activities and individuals will ensure that deadlines are met and that the project is completed with minimal disruption and without a clash of personalities.

 Test your knowledge

1 What are the stages of the project life-cycle, and how does this relate to team structure requirements?
2 Identify four factors that can impact upon the size and composition of a team.
3 Why is it important to get a good balance of team roles when working together on a project?
4 What skills should exist in order for a team to be effective?

 Exam questions

1 Large organisations often run their own system development projects, collecting a number of suitably skilled people together to form the development team.

   Describe **four** characteristics of a good IT development team. *(8 marks)*
   AQA Jan 2003

2 Explain why projects are often sub-divided into tasks and allocated to teams. *(3 marks)*
   AQA June 2003

9 Information and the professional

The use of ICT can raise a number of social, moral and ethical issues. Using technology to capture, process, store, manipulate and output information has in many cases improved operations and efficiency levels in organisations, but there are a number of issues associated with the way in which ICT is introduced and managed.

Socially, the introduction of ICT can have a negative impact on the working environment, especially if system users have not been involved in the implementation process. Some users feel threatened by technology, especially if they fear that it has been brought in as a more efficient way of doing their jobs and that their career is at risk. If system users have never used a computer before, or there is a requirement for a change in job role to accommodate the new technology, many issues can be raised.

Moral and ethical issues arise in two areas. First, there are questions about the way in which data and information are stored and used on ICT systems, in terms of:

- what data is being stored
- whether the data storage been authorised by the person who is the subject of the data
- who has the right to see and use the data.

Secondly, moral and ethical issues arise in the personal use of ICT systems by employees. Employers may take measures to monitor such use. Questions that arise include the following:

- Should employees use ICT resources for personal matters during working hours?
- Do employers have the right to monitor their employees?
- To what extent should monitoring take place?
- Do employees need to be informed of monitoring activities?

Recently new codes of practice have been drawn up relating to monitoring procedures at work, as outlined in the case study below.

Case study – Someone to watch over the office police

A new code on monitoring aims to balance an employee's right to privacy with a company's interests, writes Michael Becket

Employers should monitor workers only after telling them why and how it is to be done, according to a new code of practice from the Information Commissioner, Richard Thomas.

He said: 'Monitoring in the workplace can be intrusive, whether examining e-mails, recording phone calls, or installing CCTV cameras. Employees are entitled to expect that their personal lives remain private and they have a degree of privacy in the work environment.'

The overall aim is to strike a balance between a worker's legitimate right to respect for their private life and an employer's legitimate need to run a business, he added.

The code recommends a comprehensive assessment to see if the company really does have to monitor at all.

© Telegraph Group Limited (2003)   *Telegraph* 16 June 2003

1 Do you think that employees should be allowed to do the following during work time:
- use the telephone for personal calls
- surf the Internet
- send personal faxes and e-mails
- print out personal documents?

2 What do you consider to be acceptable monitoring?

3 Do you think that employers have the right to monitor their employees without their knowledge?

9.0 Codes of practice

All employees should understand the difference between correct and incorrect procedures and behaviour. To ensure that this distinction is upheld, and to maintain a consistent level of professionalism within the workplace, many organisations issue a code of conduct or code of practice for employees.

A code of practice is an agreement between an organisation and its ICT system's users. It contains a number of elements, such as the following:

- responsibilities for use of company hardware and software
- responsibilities for use of data
- responsibilities for the correct use of time
- responsibilities for use of the Internet or company intranet system
- authorisation in terms of security, passwords and access rights, depending on the level of the employee
- the implementation of legislation such as the Data Protection Act.

A code of conduct provides a set of guidelines about the standards and quality of work to be undertaken by employees in an organisation. It is intended to ensure that a high level of professionalism is maintained when working in the ICT industry. Codes are enforceable within organisations.

A code of conduct should outline what is acceptable within the work environment, in terms of how employees:

- carry out their job role
- interact with other employees
- present themselves professionally
- communicate with third parties.

The code should define an individual's duties to the profession, to the employer and the clients, and his or her responsibilities about levels of competence, integrity and honesty.

Codes of conduct or practice are not exclusive to employees of organisations; a range of other codes exist for members of associations, and for students attending a training or educational institute.

 Test your knowledge

1 Why should organisations have a code of practice?
2 What would a typical code of practice outline?

Exam questions

1   Discuss the social, moral and ethical issues for a professional working within the industry that might arise when introducing and using information and communication systems.

(6 marks)

AQA Jan 2003

2   **(a)** Explain what is meant by a code of practice.   *(3 marks)*

(b) Give **one** element that could be included in a code of practice, and describe the benefit that a company would gain from it.   *(3 marks)*

AQA June 2003

3   New employees joining a company are each asked to sign an agreement to adhere to a code of practice for using the organisation's computer system.

Explain **four** issues that such a code of practice should address.   *(8 marks)*

AQA June 2002

UNIT 5 – INFORMATION:
POLICY, STRATEGY AND SYSTEMS

This unit examines a range of issues connected with the ways in which data and information are used within organisations and how hardware, software and user interfaces enable this use.

The unit covers the following key areas:

- policy and strategy issues
- software: development, evaluation and reliability
- communication and ICT
- networks
- database management concepts
- HCI
- portability of data.

A range of material is used to examine each of the key areas.

1 Policy and strategy issues

Information technology (IT) policies are unique to an organisation. The majority of medium to large organisations have IT policies, their objective being to consolidate certain rules, conditions and IT strategies for the future.

Areas that may be addressed in an IT policy include:

- current hardware and software provision
- future hardware and software provision
- security and user procedural issues
- back-up
- general rules and conditions of IT usage.

All users within an organisation should be able to see from an IT policy what is expected of them in terms of IT usage, and their responsibilities in terms of following certain rules, a code of practice and legislation such as the Data Protection Act.

An IT policy may also outline current and future hardware and software provisions, so that users – especially at the tactical and strategic levels – can see how these provisions currently support the infrastructure of the organisation and the changes (if any) required for the future.

1.0 Users within an organisation

Organisations differ in size and structure. Some are considered to have a 'flat' structure with only a few layers of personnel, while others can be classified as being 'tall' or 'hierarchical', with a larger number of personnel layers (see Unit 4, pages 7–9). Typical medium-sized and large organisations will have a range of users, extending from those who work at an operational level to staff who are at the tactical-and strategic levels, as shown in the table below.

Typical users within an organisation

Operational level	Tactical level	Strategic level
Clerical and secretarial	Programmers	Directors
Manual	Analysts	Chief executives
Administrative	Knowledge workers	Senior managers
Data entry	Supervisors and middle management	

All users within an organisation will have a range of needs. Some of these will be generic (applying to all), such as access to certain resources, and hardware and software that is:

- fast and powerful
- up to date
- easy to use (for inexperienced system users)
- compatible with existing systems.

Other needs may be more specialist or even unique to a job role, for example a specific platform to run a specific piece of software.

1.1 Hardware and software provision

As technology changes and hardware and software become more sophisticated, faster and more powerful, organisations find they need to upgrade.

Upgrades can be needed because of on-going hardware or software development and change, or as part of an organisation's culture, where policy may dictate that every six or twelve months an overhaul takes place. An upgrade may also be task-driven, where higher-specification hardware or software is required to meet a specific objective.

In general an organisation may decide to upgrade to:

- ▓ sustain compatibility with existing systems
- ▓ maintain competitiveness
- ▓ ensure continued support from suppliers/vendors.

Not all organisations have the financial resources to continually upgrade their hardware and software. One way to address this is to **future proof** systems. Future proofing attempts to overcome the need to upgrade at a later date by estimating requirements in terms of storage, speed, functionality, etc. A system is purchased that incorporates a higher specification than that which is currently needed, so that it will continue to fulfil requirements in the future.

Another way to avoid the costs of upgrading hardware is to invest in **emulation software** that will allow existing hardware to act like a different type. Although this is cheaper, it does have time overheads for processing.

1.2 Back-up strategies

The consequences to an organisation of losing data can be very severe, and any disruption to processing activities can be costly and time consuming. Attempts to retrieve lost data can prove fruitless, as well as expensive.

Organisations therefore need to have a back-up strategy, and there are a number of options available.

- ▓ **Simple back-up** is the elementary type. Each time an archive is created, the oldest version of the back-up file is replaced with the newly created one.
- ▓ **Stack back-up** consists of the last created back-up together with previous versions – the previous versions being organised into a stack format.
- ▓ **Advanced back-up** differs in that it does not permit unchanged or unedited files in the old back-up copies to be stacked.
- ▓ **Incremental back-up** provides a fast method of backing up data – much faster than a full back-up. During an incremental back-up only the files that have changed since the last full or incremental back-up are included. As a result, the time taken may be a fraction of the time needed to perform a full back-up.
- ▓ **The grandfather, father, son technique** is probably the most common back-up method. It uses a rotation set of back-up disks or tapes so that three different versions of the same data are held at any one time. An example of this method is shown in Figure 1.

Figure 1

Grandfather, father, son back-up method

Customer order data					
Monday		**Tuesday**		**Wednesday**	
Disk 1	Grandfather	Disk 2	Grandfather	Disk 3	Grandfather
Disk 2	Father	Disk 3	Father	Disk 1	Father
Disk 3	Son	Disk 1	Son	Disk 2	Son

Back-up strategies are essential, and apply to both home users and business users. On a corporate level, the stakes are that much higher in terms of potentially losing valuable information.

The steps involved with and issues surrounding back-up are quite simple. First, data needs to be 'dumped' or 'transferred' from a live system to the chosen back-up medium. In terms of capacity, the media type – for example tape – may offer a limited amount of space. Therefore consideration needs to be given to:

- the frequency of the data dumps – will they be complete or incremental?
- who or what will be responsible for switching over the media when full
- time issues – how long the process will take. Can the back-up be done during office hours, or is it restricted to overnight?

The second step to consider is that of verifying the storage media. If possible, the back-up software should verify the data as it is written to the tape. Otherwise, a process of checking should be instituted after a certain number of back-ups to make sure the data is as required.

Correct data storage is also essential, and steps should be taken to ensure that:

- at the very least there is a fireproof safe for tapes
- if the organisation is split between multiple buildings or sites, a process is in place for moving tapes to remote locations, working on the principle that two offices are unlikely to burn down together
- another secure off-site location for storing back-ups is considered, to deter any attempts to damage data deliberately.

A third step in a back-up strategy is to ensure that if data is lost, recovery can take place as soon as possible. This means immediate access is needed to the back-up medium, together with knowledge of how to initiate the recovery process.

The implementation of the policy and process can be considered the last stage in any back-up strategy. Documenting what, when, where and by whom back-ups and recovery have taken place is crucial – maintaining accurate records and ensuring that people are aware of this strategy will ensure that tasks are implemented correctly.

First National Bank of Scotia have opted for an off-site back-up facility with Sanbolic (http://www.sanbolic.com) – see the next page.

The Storage Area Network (SAN) that has been used provides the following benefits:

- protection from hardware failures
- increased speed
- storage flexibility (on how data is stored and data recovery).

The service that has been provided will accommodate their own strategy and support their need to back-up their on-line banking system nightly to an off-site location.

First National Bank of Scotia
Case Study

The Challenge

First National Bank of Scotia needed to update their online banking system with a more secure, automated backup procedure. The bank wanted to implement a cost effective solution, less susceptible to regional disasters, such as primary and backup sites going offline. Chris Welch, former Network Administrator, was asked to analyze these requirements and provide a solution flexible enough to be easily incorporated into the existing infrastructure of the online banking system. The primary requirements were to fully utilize existing storage space, better manage the data shared between the servers and increase the speed of recovery if data went offline.

First National Bank of Scotia decided that a Storage Area Network was the best solution. The redundancy built into a SAN would protect the bank from hardware failures, and increase the speed of the servers. A SAN provided flexibility on how data was stored between the existing servers and made data recovery possible, without taking the systems offline to reallocate storage among the LUNs. In event of hardware failure, the bank wanted SQL servers in the SAN to handle critical applications, alleviating the cost and complexity of typical fail-over solutions, which require redundant hardware and storage replication. The bank needed a fail-proof solution to manage the SAN.

The Solution

Melio FS enables all four servers to share applications on the SAN while utilizing a single terabyte LUN. All servers can access critical files and share data without partitioning an inflexible LUN for each server, providing control and stability to the SAN.

The National Bank of Scotia backs up their online banking system nightly and sends data over Ethernet to an off-site location. This data is stored on a large NAS box that is moved weekly to a secondary backup, which is removed from the network for secure storage.

"Being able to share storage among four servers means that I can buy a large amount of storage and not have to worry about which system will fill up first; unless the entire volume fills up I shouldn't have to worry about storage at all" says James J. Smith. "In addition, having one LUN (logical unit) makes the entire SAN simple to backup to disk over either fibre channel or Ethernet without interrupting other processes. Melio FS makes this possible for us."

Back-up strategies will protect data from a range of mishaps, including:

- accidental changes to or deletion of data
- loss of data due to media or software faults
- virus infections
- hackers
- catastrophic events such as fire or flood.

Any back-up strategy needs to take decisions about the following.

- **Frequency.** To ensure that back-ups remain up to date, they should be carried out regularly. The greater the frequency with which data is changed, the more frequently back-ups should be made. If data is changing significantly every day, daily back-ups are necessary.
- **Multiple copies.** As well as backing up frequently, several back-up copies should be made at different dates in case a problem arises in a working copy.
- **Off-site backup.** Some back-up copies should be stored in a separate location to safeguard against serious threats such as fire or physical disasters.
- **Media.** Back-up copies should be made on new media. Problems could occur if storage media are used more than once, as faults could begin to develop. For example, floppy disks

are not a good medium for back-up copies. If they are used, they should be replaced often. Back-up copies should also be stored on multiple media (e.g. zip disk and CD Rom) to avoid all back-up copies becoming corrupted by the same drive or disk fault.

Test your knowledge

1 Why might the IT needs of the following categories of users change within an organisation?
   - ▩ sales data entry clerk
   - ▩ sales manager
   - ▩ finance assistant
   - ▩ programmer.
2 Why would the IT needs of users differ depending on whether they operated at an operational, tactical or strategic level?
3 Why might it be necessary for an organisation to regularly update its hardware and software provision?
4 What is meant by the term *future proofing*, and what steps can an organisation take to embrace this?
5 Identify three different back-up strategies and give a description of each.

Exam questions

1 Describe **four** factors that need to be considered when a large company is devising a back-up strategy for its information systems.   *(8 marks)*
                                                                                      AQA Jan 2003

2 Hardware and software are often described as being 'compatible' with other hardware and software.

   (a) Describe the term *compatible* in this context.   *(2 marks)*
   (b) An emulator can sometimes be used to achieve compatibility.
   Describe **one** advantage and **one** limitation of the use of emulation.   *(4 marks)*
                                                                                      AQA Jan 2003

3 A graphic designer makes use of a particular hardware platform and particular software packages. Her clients often send her files produced on computer systems that are incompatible with hers. One solution for the designer is to use emulation software. Describe **one** advantage and **one** limitation the designer will have if she pursues this solution.   *(4 marks)*
                                                                                      AQA June 2002

2 **Software**

Software can be categorised into three main areas:

- operating system software
- applications software
- utility software.

Operating system software interacts with the hardware of the computer to ensure that the system resources are managed, controlled and co-ordinated. Operating system software is used on both stand-alone and networked systems and can be described as being text- or graphics-based. An example of a text-based operating system is MS DOS, and graphics-based systems include Windows 2000 and Windows XP.

Applications software allows users to carry out information processing activities, such as:

- word processing
- numerical and financial modelling and statistical analysis
- desk-top publishing
- document management, presentation, storage, retrieval and manipulation.

Applications software also enables users to interact with hardware through different text, sound, animation, video and communication techniques.

Utility software provides the tools to support the operation and management of the system. Examples include:

- virus checkers
- security software, e.g. firewalls
- defragmenter software
- partitioning software
- CD authoring
- DVD playback software.

2.0 **Evaluation of software**

When choosing software of any description it is wise to carry out an evaluation to ensure that it is **fit for purpose**. Organisations will almost always undertake a software evaluation to ensure that it:

- meets the need of the end user/customer
- meets the task objectives
- falls within an agreed budget
- is compatible with other existing hardware and software
- is upgradeable.

2.1 **Evaluation criteria**

Some organisations produce an evaluation checklist when acquiring new software. The selection criteria can include a number of the following:

- **Suitability for an agreed problem specification.** The acquisition of software can be triggered by the need to meet an agreed problem specification, for example the purchasing of an accounts package to assist system users with cash-flow, capital-spend or budget-control issues. The problem could be triggered at an individual level, with a system user needing support in his or her job role, at a functional level to support a department such as sales or accounts, or at an organisational level.

- **Functionality.** When software is purchased, consideration needs to be given to the system users and the environment in which the tasks are to be carried out. Failure to acknowledge these could result in the software being too complex, too inflexible or inappropriate for the tasks it was acquired for.

  Software that is not functionally suited to either the users or task requirements could prove to be costly in the short and long term. In the short term an organisation may have to pay for additional user training to enable it to use the software, and in the long term an organisation might need a complete software overhaul to ensure that all requirements are met.

- **Performance and robustness.** It is essential that the software acquired is fit for purpose. Software that cannot be used is a costly and redundant resource.

- **Usability and human/computer interface.** How easy is it for a user to work with the software? Key considerations when acquiring software include:
  - levels and types of users
  - nature of tasks
  - type of interface
  - built-in help screens, menus, search facilities, etc.

- **Compatibility with existing software.** A primary consideration when acquiring new software is its compatibility with existing software or hardware platforms. Depending upon the size of the organisation, a number of systems may already exist, and any new software purchased will have to be compatible to facilitate the transfer of data and to ensure end users can access data stored.

- **Ease of data transfer between software and systems.** The ease of data transfer is an issue to consider, because during the implementation of the new software, data may need to be downloaded or transferred to the new software. This links with compatibility – if the new software is not compliant with existing systems, data transfer may be delayed or impossible.

- **User support offered and integrated with the software.** The amount of user support that is available could influence an organisation's decisions when acquiring software. User support could be integrated within the software or supplied through the use of manuals, step-by-step guides, tutorials or support services provided by the supplier.

- **Additional resource requirements**, for example hardware, software, staff, equipment. When acquiring new software other resources may also have to be reviewed and possibly upgraded. These resources may include hardware that provides faster processing speed, more storage or more memory. Additional human resources may also be required to implement or maintain the software, and also to train users of the software.

- **Ease of upgrading.** Upgrading to newer software versions or replacing an entire software suite can be costly in terms of time and money. The ease of upgrading software may influence an organisation's choice. For example, rather than changing between software brands it may be easier to upgrade software within the same brand for a newer version.

- **Portability.** Another consideration when acquiring software is the portability of data – how easy will it be to transfer data between software and system types? Will there be any conflicts or compatibility issues to resolve?
- **Costs.** Finally, an organisation will always consider the costs involved. These costs can range from the purchase costs to training, acquisition of new hardware, site licences and so on.

The decision to acquire and select software can be modelled as a seven-step process.

1 Analyse needs – why is the software required, and what objectives will be met?
2 Specify requirements – factors include:
   - compatibility with existing systems, hardware and software
   - cost constraints
   - user issues – how user friendly the software needs to be
   - the level of interaction desired
   - the amount of documentation required
   - technical support required.
3 Select a range of software.
4 Draw up a shortlist of suitable software.
5 Preview software. Select users to test the software to check whether it meets the organisation's needs (software evaluation).
6 Make recommendations to acquire the software.
7 Obtain post-use feedback from system users.

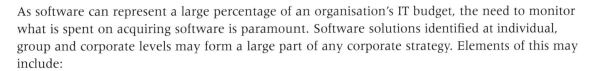

An important stage in selecting software is to obtain feedback from users who have tried it

As software can represent a large percentage of an organisation's IT budget, the need to monitor what is spent on acquiring software is paramount. Software solutions identified at individual, group and corporate levels may form a large part of any corporate strategy. Elements of this may include:

- buying only the software that is required by users and ensuring that it is used effectively
- using only licensed software and undertaking regular audits to ensure that any systems do not have illegal software installed on them
- upgrading as opposed to overhauling – it may be more cost effective to move to a more recent version of the same software than to overhaul to a different piece of software
- planning all software purchases and upgrades systematically
- working within an agreed budget.

2.2 Evaluation report

The software evaluation report will include:

- methodologies used
- recommendations
- the evaluation itself
- justifications.

A number of methods may be used to collect information about all alternative software. Questions such as the following can be put to users at all levels:

- How often do you expect to use the software?
- How would the software support you in your tasks/job role?
- How easy is it to use the software?
- What problems have you encountered?

Information could be collected through the use of questionnaires, interviewing, focus groups or by observing how users interact with the software.

The evaluation involves collating all the responses given in order to analyse the feedback. The evaluation could be broken down into sections, such as:

- evaluation of software use
- evaluation of software functionality
- evaluation of resources required to support the software.

Each offered solution is assessed against requirements and graded. Each requirement or criterion is given a different weighting and an overall score can be calculated.

The recommendations and justifications provide the opportunity to put forward objective statements about the findings and to offer solutions to address any problems identified by users, if appropriate. The opportunity also exists to explain why problems exist, or why users were happy with software. The recommendations might clearly identify the ideal solution or might indicate the need to upgrade to a newer software version, train end users or to extend the software to other parts of the organisation (especially if the software evaluation report was based on a pilot of the software in one functional area).

Control and monitoring of the software acquisition process is vital and can save time and money, improve employee productivity and ensure IT compatibility throughout the organisation. Controlling and monitoring software can also assist in organisational change – making it easier to bring about change.

Test your knowledge

1 Why is it important for an organisation to carry out an evaluation of its software requirements?
2 What issues should be addressed when evaluating software?
3 The decision to acquire and select software can be modelled on a seven-step process. Provide a brief overview of each of the steps.

Exam questions

1 A large market research company is considering several different software packages in order to assist with the analysis of data collected on behalf of clients.

Give **three** criteria that should be considered when evaluating these software packages. For each criterion, explain why it may be important to this company. *(9 marks)*

AQA June 2002

2 Give **four** reasons for producing an evaluation report when considering alternative software solutions to a particular problem. *(4 marks)*

AQA Jan 2003

3 Database management concepts

A relational database management system (DBMS) is the software that allows an organisation to centralise its data, thus providing an efficient, accessible and secure environment for stored data through the use of application programs. A relational DBMS acts as an interface between application programs and the data files, as illustrated in Figure 2.

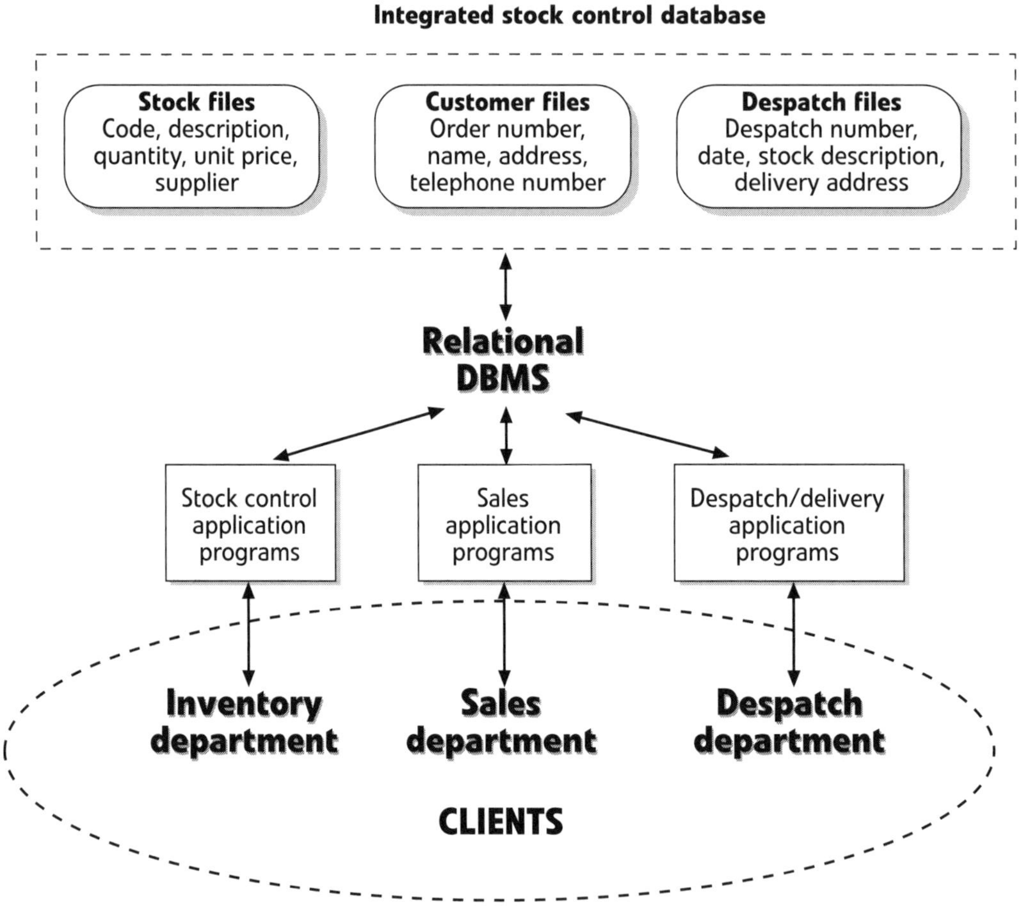

Integrated stock control database

Figure 2

Relational DBMS stock control environment on a client/server database

3.0 Components of a relational database management system

There are three major components to a relational DBMS:

- data definition language
- data manipulation language
- data dictionary.

The **data definition language** (DDL) is the formal language used by programmers to specify the content and structure of the database. DDL is a descriptive language that is used to outline the entities required for the application, and the relationships that may exist between them.

The **data manipulation language** (DML) is a specialised language that is used in conjunction with other generation programming languages to manipulate the data within the database. The language contains commands that allow system users and programmers to extract data from the database in order to carry out user requests and enable applications development. The most prominent DML is Structured Query Language (SQL).

The final component of a relational DBMS is the **data dictionary**. This is an automated or manual file that stores definitions of data elements and characteristics such as usage, ownership, authorisation and security. Many data dictionaries can produce lists and reports of data utilisation, groupings, program locations and so on. Most data dictionaries are passive; they simply report. With more advanced types, a change in the dictionary is automatically used by any related programs. For example, to change a telephone number from six to eight digits, you would simply enter the change in the dictionary without having to modify and recompile all of the application programs using telephone numbers.

3.1 Functions of a relational database management system

Codd (1982) identifies a number of functions and services that a full-scale relational DBMS should provide. These include the following.

- Data storage, retrieval and update – fundamental functions of a relational DBMS.
- User-accessible catalogue/data dictionary – a repository information system that describes the data within the database.
- Transaction support – ensuring that any actions carried out on the database are consistent by updating all or none of them.
- Concurrency control services – ensuring that the database is updated correctly when multiple users are updating the database simultaneously.
- Authorisation services – allowing only authorised users access to the database.
- Recovery services – mechanisms for recovering the database in the event of an accident.
- Data communication support – the ability to integrate with communication software.
- Integrity services – mechanisms to ensure that the data and any changes made to the data in the database follow certain rules.
- Services that promote data independence – facilities that support the independence of programs from the structure of the database.
- Utility services – including utility programs, for example monitoring import facilities and statistical programs.

3.2 Benefits and limitations of a relational DBMS

Database management systems, like any software, have a range of benefits and limitations. These are shown in the table below.

Benefits of relational DBMS		Limitations of relational DBMS	
Manages data redundancy more effectively than file-based systems:	Integration of files reduces duplication of data	Complexity:	The level of functionality expected makes the RDBMS quite complex
Improved security:	Ability to set up security measures, e.g. passwords, to restrict user entry	Costs:	Associated costs include updating hardware, training, staffing, security
Data consistency:	By managing data redundancy, inconsistencies are greatly reduced	Greater impact if system fails:	By centralising resources, any problems have a wider impact
Sharing of data:	Centralised approach allows multiple user access to shared data resources	Reduced performance:	In comparison to a specialist file-based system, a DBMS is more generalised
Addresses internal conflict requirements between functional departments:	No single department would have ownership of the data – there is equal access		

For many organisations, the main advantage of a relational DBMS would be its ability to centralise, share and reduce data redundancy. The main disadvantage would be the cost of maintaining it.

Data integrity

What does this mean?

Data integrity: The correctness of the data.

The integrity of data can be compromised in a number of ways. These include:

- human errors when data is entered, and errors that occur when data is transmitted from one computer to another
- software bugs or viruses

- hardware malfunctions, such as disk crashes
- natural disasters, such as fires and floods.

To counteract these threats, a number of steps can be taken:

- backing up data regularly
- controlling access to data via security mechanisms
- designing user interfaces that prevent the input of invalid data
- using error detection and correction software when transmitting data.

Data redundancy

Data redundancy is a problem that can occur when data is stored electronically. Data can be duplicated in a number of different places, therefore making some redundant.

Data consistency

Data consistency is a major requirement for all databases, but particularly for those that are distributed. If data redundancy is well managed, inconsistencies are greatly reduced.

Data independence

The process of data independence separates the data from the programs that use it. Nearly all modern applications are based on the principle of data independence, and the whole concept of relational DBMS supports the notion of data independence, since it is a system for managing data separately from the programs that use it.

3.3 Database users and the role of the database administrator

There are a number of roles that are associated with a database environment. People who take on these roles vary in expertise from novices using the databases to technical experts who design and mould the system.

The database environment extends from procedures and standards, to systems software, including application programs, operating systems and DBMS, through to the hardware. At each point in this environment there is some input from people, ensuring that:

- the database is correctly designed to agreed specifications
- programs are written in accordance with end-user needs
- the user interface is designed for the needs of the end user
- the data, storage and manipulation facilities are accessible
- the database is running correctly
- the software and hardware supporting the database system are compatible and are operating without conflicts.

The people involved with this process include analysts, programmers, designers, database administrators, system administrators and end users. Collectively they ensure that the database performs to its specification.

Analyst	→	Identifies the initial need for and feasibility of a database within a given environment
Programmer	→	Works within the boundaries of a given specification to ensure that the database is functional for the end user
Designer	→	Identifies the data and constraints on the data that is to be stored, and takes the logical data model and decides how it can be physically executed
Database administrator	→	Manages and controls the RDBMS and its data – responsible for the data resource, security, and the development and maintenance of standards and policies
System administrator	→	Manages and controls the hardware that supports the RDBMS. Responsible for upgrades, back-up and recovery procedures and risk management
End user	→	Uses the database to store and process data and information

3.4 RDBMS software

There is a range of software that supports the functions of an RDBMS. The major ones are:

- Oracle
- IBM with DB2
- Informix
- Microsoft with SQL Server.

However, the traditional RDBMS is being challenged by the newer object-orientated RDBMS such as O2, Object Store and Objectivity.

3.5 Entity relationships

Entity relationship diagrams (ERDs) are used to provide an overview of the main data sets or entities within a given system. Entities are objects that can include people, events or places. For example, in a school enrolment system entities could include:

- students
- lecturers
- qualifications.
- applications
- courses

Within a system each entity occurrence is linked to one or many other entities. This link is a relationship that can be identified as being one of the following.

One to one (1:1)

This denotes that only one occurrence of each entity is used by the adjoining entity.

A lecturer teachers on a course.

One to many (1:M)

This denotes that a single occurrence of one entity is linked to more than one occurrence of the adjoining entity.

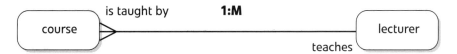

A lecturer teaches on more than one course.

Many to many (M:N)

This denotes that many occurrences of one entity are linked to more than one occurrence of the adjoining entity.

A lecturer teaches on more than one course, and a course is taught by more than one lecturer.

Although M:N relationships are common, the notation of linking two entities directly is adjusted and a link entity is used to connect the two, so that:

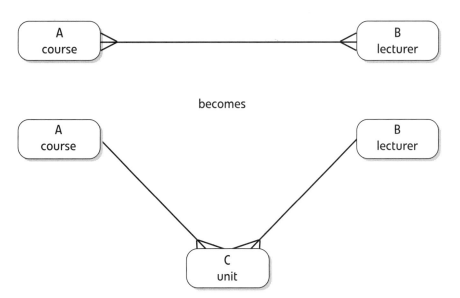

Attributes

Each entity has a set of attributes that describe some aspects of it that are to be recorded, for example:

Entity: Course
Attributes: Course code
                 Title
                 Mode
                 Start date
                 End date

Each set of attributes within that entity should have a unique field that provides easy identification with the entity type. In the case of the entity type 'course', the unique key field is that of the 'Course code'. The unique field or **primary key** will ensure that although two courses may have similar titles, the course code will differentiate the two.

3.6 Data normalisation

Normalisation is a bottom-up approach to database design that starts by examining relationships between attributes. The initial framework is modelled on three stages or tests that are applied to a given 'relation'. These stages are called:

- first normal form (1NF) – remove repeating groups
- second normal form (2NF) – remove partial key dependencies
- third normal form (3NF) – remove non-key dependencies.

An example of normalising data up to third normal form is shown below.

Unnormalised data set

*Student number	Student name	Module code	Module name	Grade number	Lecturer	Room
CP123/OP	Greene	C122	IS	D	Jenkins	B33
CP938/CP	Jacobs	C123	Hardware	M	Smith	B33
CF489/LP	Browne	C124	Software	M	Osborne	B32
CP311/CP	Peters	C111	Internet	P	Chives	B32
CR399/CP	Porter	C110	Web design	D	Crouch	B33
CD478/JP	Graham	C107	Multimedia	M	Waters	B31
CR678/LP	Denver	C106	Networking	P	Rowan	B31

Primary key

Converting an unnormalised data set (UNF) into first normal form (1NF) involves looking at the structure. To do this, the data needs to be divided into two:

1 fixed part
2 variable part that contains repetitions.

To rejoin the data the variable part must contain a key from the fixed part to make a composite key of Student number/Module code, as shown on the next page.

First normal form (1NF)

Student number	Student name
CP123/OP	Greene
CP938/CP	Jacobs
CF489/LP	Browne
CP311/CP	Peters
CR399/CP	Porter
CD478/JP	Graham
CR678/LP	Denver

Student number	Module code	Module name	Grade	Lecturer	Room number
CP123/OP	C122	IS	D	Jenkins	B33
CP938/CP	C123	Hardware	M	Smith	B33
CF489/LP	C124	Software	M	Osborne	B32
CP311/CP	C111	Internet	P	Chives	B32
CR399/CP	C110	Web design	D	Crouch	B33
CD478/JP	C107	Multimedia	M	Waters	B31
CR678/LP	C106	Networking	P	Rowan	B31

The 1NF should be examined for any partial dependencies that exist within the data set.

For example, Module name is derived from Module code (it makes no difference which student is taking that module).

However, the grade is not partially dependant because it is the grade for an individual student taking a particular module.

Problems with partial dependence include the following.

■ Updating – if for example the name of module C124 (Software) changed to 'Operating systems', every record that contained the old module details would need to be updated.

■ Insert anomaly – under the current organisation, module details such as its name are stored with records about individual students taking that module. A new module would have no students enrolled onto it, so where would it be stored?

■ Deletion anomaly – if a student decides to drop a module or leave the course, all the details of that module will be lost.

Second normal form (2NF)

Student number	Student name
CP123/OP	Greene
CP938/CP	Jacobs
CF489/LP	Browne
CP311/CP	Peters
CR399/CP	Porter
CD478/JP	Graham
CR678/LP	Denver

Student number	Module code	Grade
CP123/OP	C122	D
CP938/CP	C123	M
CF489/LP	C124	M
CP311/CP	C111	P
CR399/CP	C110	D
CD478/JP	C107	M
CR678/LP	C106	P

Module code	Module name	Lecturer	Room number
C122	IS	Jenkins	B33
C123	Hardware	Smith	B33
C124	Software	Osborne	B32
C111	Internet	Chives	B32
C110	Web design	Crouch	B33
C107	Multimedia	Waters	B31
C106	Networking	Rowan	B31

The next step is to ensure that the data does not show any indirect dependencies. All non-key fields should be defined by the key directly and not by another non-key field.

For example, the room number is defined by the lecturer and not by the module. This creates similar dependency problems of updating, and insertion and deletion anomalies.

- If a lecturer moves to another room, the room location would also need to be changed.
- A lecturer not allocated to teaching a module cannot have any room details stored.
- If a lecturer stops teaching a module the room details will be lost.

To overcome these problems further divisions in the data structure are required.

Third normal form (3NF)

Student number	Student name
CP123/OP	Greene
CP938/CP	Jacobs
CF489/LP	Browne
CP311/CP	Peters
CR399/CP	Porter
CD478/JP	Graham
CR678/LP	Denver

Student number	Module code	Grade
CP123/OP	C122	D
CP938/CP	C123	M
CF489/LP	C124	M
CP311/CP	C111	P
CR399/CP	C110	D
CD478/JP	C107	M
CR678/LP	C106	P

Lecturer	Room number
Jenkins	B33
Smith	B33
Osborne	B32
Chives	B32
Crouch	B33
Waters	B31
Rowan	B31

Module code	Module name	Lecturer
C122	IS	Jenkins
C123	Hardware	Smith
C124	Software	Osborne
C111	Internet	Chives
C110	Web design	Crouch
C107	Multimedia	Waters
C106	Networking	Rowan

Test your knowledge

1 What are the components of a DBMS?
2 Identify three benefits and limitations of using DBMS.
3 Outline some of the responsibilities of a database administrator.
4 What are the components of an entity relationship diagram? Provide an example of each component in the following systems:
   - college system
   - hospital
   - car rental system.
5 What is the function of normalisation, and what are the distinctions between UNF, 1NF, 2NF and 3NF?

Exam questions

1 **(a)** Explain what is meant by a *relational database management system.* *(3 marks)*

(b) A successful relational database will have undergone normalisation.
Describe what is meant by *normalisation.* *(2 marks)*

AQA Jan 2003

2 The secretary of a local tennis club is constructing a database to store data on members' personal details and records of attendance. He has been told that a relational database management system can assist him. Having found an article on relational database construction, he does not understand some of the terminology it contains. He asks you for advice.

(a) Explain the following terms:
(i) normalisation
(ii) data independence
(iii) data consistency
(iv) data integrity. *(8 marks)*

(b) The secretary constructs his database structure and asks you to examine his work before he enters any data. You notice that he has not included any validation.
With the aid of an example, explain why data validation is important. *(3 marks)*

(c) Give **three** reasons why he should consult with other members of the tennis club committee before finalising the design of the database system. *(3 marks)*

AQA June 2002

4 Communication and information systems

A networked system can bring many benefits to an organisation. Some of these include:

- sharing of data and information, and the dissemination of good practice
- increased efficiency
- sharing of resources, e.g. printers and scanners
- reducing information transfer time
- reducing costs.

As a result of these benefits, many organisations opt for a networked solution – despite the financial outlay, the set-up costs, the possible disruption to employees, and the need to train and update.

Networks have enabled organisations to access a range of business solutions through the use of different types of software applications and communication tools, more specifically the growth in 'groupware' tools such as:

- e-mail
- voicemail
- teleconferencing and videoconferencing
- facsimile (fax servers for desktop fax)
- collaboration/workgroup software.

The setting up of intranets, extranets, bulletin boards, newsgroups and the use of the Internet have enabled organisations to become more competitive and more flexible in their business practices.

E-mail is the transmission of messages across a communication network. The popularity of e-mail has risen due to the speed with which messages can be transmitted, the ability to share data and to send multiple copies. Other advantages of e-mail include its low cost in relation to using other communication media, the ability to attach a range of multimedia to text documents (pictures, movie clips, hyperlinks, etc.), and its auditing facilities – users can store messages sent and received, track documents by date, time and author, and also generate receipts.

Voicemail provides users with the option of setting up a recorded message on the telephone and using audio tape to capture information that may have been lost if the recipient was not available to take a call.

Conferencing applications include text, white boarding and more commonly videoconferencing. Conferencing facilities allow users to communicate interactively over a set distance.

Facsimile systems transmit an image through a telephone connection. Faxes can be sent through a conventional fax machine or through a fax modem.

Videoconferencing allows users to hold a 'face-to-face' meeting at a distance

Collaboration software provides the opportunity for groups of users to interact within a secure environment. Collaboration could take the form of an on-line discussion, verbal communication via a microphone, or active participation in the creation or editing of documents.

4.0 Networks

Networks vary in size and complexity. Some are used in a single department or office, and others extend across local, national or international branches. Networks vary in structure, to accommodate the need to exchange information across small or large geographical areas. These structures include:

- local area networks (LANs)
- metropolitan area network (MANs)
- wide area networks (WANs) – long haulage networks (LHNs)
- value added networks (VANs).

Local area networks

These consist of computers located physically close to each other – within the same department or branch. A typical structure would include a set of computers and peripherals linked as individual nodes. Each node, for example a computer and shared peripheral, is directly connected by cables that serve as a pathway for transferring data between machines. See Figure 3.

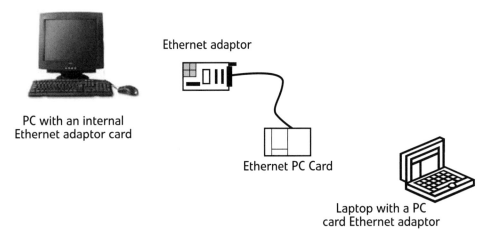

PC with an internal
Ethernet adaptor card

Ethernet adaptor

Ethernet PC Card

Laptop with a PC
card Ethernet adaptor

Figure 3
Typical local area network

Metropolitan area networks

These are more efficient than a LAN and use fibre optic cables to allow more information and a higher complexity of information. The range of a MAN is also greater than a LAN, allowing business to expand around a large city, for example – hence the name 'metropolitan'. However, this can prove to be expensive because of the fibre optic cabling.

Wide area networks/long haulage networks

These are networks that extend over a larger geographical distance, from city to city within the same country or across countries and even continents. WANs transfer data between LANs on a back-bone system using digital, satellite or even microwave technology. A WAN will connect different servers at a site. When this connection is from a PC on one site to a server on another, it is referred to as being **remote**. If this coverage is international, it is referred to as an **enterprise-wide** network.

Value added networks

This type of network is a data network that has all the benefits of a WAN but with vastly reduced costs. The cost of setting up and maintaining this type of network is reduced because the service provider rents out the network to different companies, as opposed to an organisation having sole ownership or a 'point-to-point' private line.

The use of networks

Networks can be used to support a range of applications within an organisation, the selection of a particular network depending on:

- the application or use
- the number of users requiring access
- physical resources
- the scope of the network – within a room, department, across departments or branches.

If, for example, a network was required to link a few computers within the same department to enable the sharing of certain resources, a LAN might be installed. If a network was required to link branches and supplier sources across the country, a WAN might be installed, with the server located at the head office providing remote access to users connecting at individual branches.

Internet infrastructure

The Internet is probably the most well-known network system – every computer that is connected to the Internet is part of this network.

The Internet uses interconnected providers at **network access points** (NAPs) across the globe. Terabytes of data flow between the individual networks at these points. The Internet is therefore a large collection of corporate networks that all communicate with each other at the NAPs. All of these networks rely on NAPs, backbones and routers to talk to each other.

Routers determine where to send the information from one computer to another. They are specialised computers that send messages quickly to their destinations along thousands of pathways.

Routers determine the best path for sending information, and have a switching function between networks

A router serves two purposes. First it ensures that information doesn't go astray by determining the best path to use – this is crucial for keeping large volumes of data from clogging up connections. Secondly it has a switching function, to move from one network to another.

A router is invaluable in these two roles. It joins networks together, passing information from one to another, and also protects networks from each other – it prevents the traffic from one unnecessarily spilling over to another. Regardless of how many networks are attached, the basic operation and function of the router remains the same. Since the Internet is one huge network made up of tens of thousands of smaller networks, the use of routers is an absolute necessity.

In order to handle all the users of even a large private network, millions and millions of data packets must be sent at the same time. Some of the largest routers are made by Cisco Systems Inc.

These routers use the same sort of design as some of the most powerful supercomputers; this design links many different processors together with a series of extremely fast switches.

ROUTING SOLUTIONS FOR SERVICE PROVIDERS

December 10, 2003: Cisco Scales the Core and Delivers Services at the Edge

Scaling the Core, Delivering Services at the Edge

Cisco delivers the industry's first field upgradeable 40 Gigabit core routing solution on the Cisco 12000 Series Router – doubling the capacity of the world's largest IP/MPLS networks without a forklift upgrade. Cisco sharpens carrier service delivery with innovative service capabilities at the network edge powered by the Cisco 7600 Series and 12000 Series routers.

With a continued reduction in infrastructure budgets service, providers need to simplify and consolidate their networks – not only to lower capital expenses but reduce operational expenses. Additionally the drive to replace lost revenues is creating the opportunity for carriers to implement premium services above and beyond traditional connectivity.

Cisco is meeting the demands of their carrier customers by delivering significant advancements in service provider core and edge routing solutions.

Servers

All of the machines on the Internet are either servers or clients. The machines that provide services to other machines are servers, and the machines that are used to connect to those services are clients. Servers can be categorised into the following:

- web servers
- file transfer protocol (FTP) servers
- e-mail servers
- newsgroup servers.

When you connect to a website to read a page, you are accessing that site's web server.

The server machine finds the page you requested and sends it to you. Clients come to a server machine for a specific purpose, so they direct their requests to a specific software server running on the server machine.

4.1 Distributed systems

Distributed databases consist of two or more data files that are each located in different areas on a network. As a result, different users can access the data sets without disrupting other users.

The use of a distributed database system can create a number of issues – some are positive, and others negative. The advantages of using a distributed database include the following:

- **Reliability and availability:** because of the distributed element, if one part of the database crashes or fails it will not disable the entire database – other data sets in other areas can still be accessed.
- **Autonomy of data:** users at one site can have control over their own data.
- **Growth/expansion:** this type of system can be expanded to incorporate more data sets in other areas of the network.

The disadvantages of using a distributed database include the following.

- **Cost:** in terms of set-up charges, installation, hardware and software.
- **Complexity:** setting up a distributed database, ensuring that all data sets can be accessed.
- **Security:** controlling and monitoring the network and data control issues.
- **Reliance on telecommunications:** the system will not function if telecommunications fail.
- **Management overhead/staff costs:** these can be high.

Case study

This case study outlines some of the disadvantages of distributed databases and the way forward for distributed computing.

DATAMATION ®   ● EARTHWEB·

Distributed databases, distributed headaches

By Karen D. Schwartz   http://products.datamation.com

Chuck Shellhouse knows really big databases. Shellhouse, the Colorado Springs-based director of service operations in the information technology division of MCI, is responsible for managing more than 40 terabytes of data located in datacentres around the country. Those databases, which primarily run DB2 and Adabas on IBM and Hitachi mainframes, contain all of the business applications needed to run the telecommunications company's entire $20+ billion revenue stream.

Even though MCI's database dwarfs the databases of most corporations, MCI's computing model has become increasingly common. With companies generating and keeping more data to make better decisions on how to make money, many organisations now rely on the model of geographically dispersed, multiterabyte databases.

But today's forward-thinking companies are changing the definition of distributed computing. No longer are they managing hundreds of distributed environments running small servers. By and large, they've found such set-ups, which involve installing software and backing up data at each location, to be time-consuming and expensive.

Instead, these companies have consolidated their data into just a few datacentres, housing much larger amounts of data at each centre. At MCI, Shellhouse and his staff used to manage numerous datacentres in many locations around the country. But with managerial problems and costs spiralling – the datacentres required on-site support personnel, operational personnel, and systems programmers at each location – Shellhouse and his team devised a plan to replace those datacentres with 'megacentres' on the backbone of MCI's network. Today, the company has just four datacentres.

Consolidating a dozen datacentres into a few makes a lot of sense for most large companies, says Daniel Graham, a Somers, N.Y.-based strategy and operations executive in IBM's Global Business Intelligence Solutions group.

'Having [distributed datacentres] is like having children. Two are wonderful, four are a lot of fun, six start to be a drain on your resources, and 20 are impossible,' Graham says. 'Every time you have another child, you have bought yourself a certain amount of overhead cost.'

The Internet: a new paradigm

Database experts have seen the future of distributed computing, and it is the Internet. The Internet provides IT managers with an easier mechanism for distributing data to end users. By simplifying and consolidating on one universal client, they can contact their customers and work with their business partners much more easily.

The Internet changes the whole paradigm of distributed computing, says Carl Olofson, research director for database management systems at International Data Corp., the Framingham, Mass., consulting firm.

'Ultimately, instead of an organisation having a fixed topology of networks that have to be connected together, they can employ a much more flexible scheme using the Internet instead of allowing regional offices to connect through their system,' Olofson says. In addition, the Internet enables companies to connect to each other and create virtual enterprises, he notes.

1 Identify the problems that MCI encountered by consolidating its data into datacentres.

2 How did MCI address these problems?

3 What role does the Internet play in terms of distributed computing?

Distributed database systems also allow applications to be accessed from local and remote databases. The two types of system are:

- homogenous distributed database systems
- heterogeneous distributed database systems.

In a **homogenous** distributed database system the network consists of two or more databases of the same type that exist on one or more machines. An application can therefore simultaneously access or modify the data in several databases, as shown in Figure 4 on the next page, illustrating four databases and their related clients. The underlying technology to support this is referred to as 'clustering'. Homogenous databases all use the same relational (RDBMS) software and have the same applications on each computer.

In a **heterogeneous** distributed database system, the architecture is the same as shown in Figure 4, but at least one of the databases is of a different type. Heterogeneous databases have a high degree of local autonomy – each computer has its own local users, applications and data, and only connects to other computers on the network for the information that it does not have. This type of distributed database is also referred to as a **federated system.**

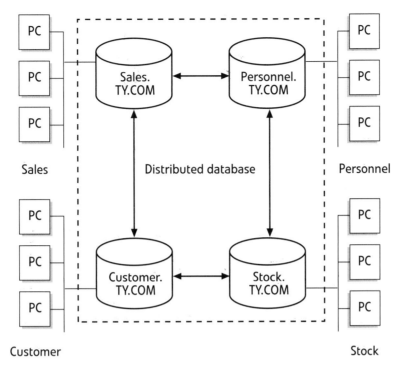

Figure 4

Example of a distributed system

4.2 **Client/server systems**

The client/server approach is based on a client that processes requests for data and a server that executes the request and returns results, as shown in Figure 5.

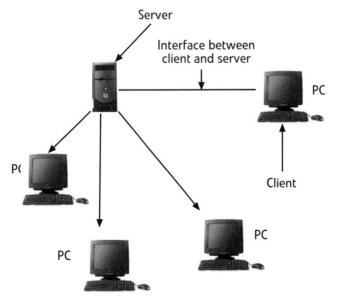

Figure 5

Example of a client/server

The server is a more powerful computer that stores the application and the data shared by users. It effectively circulates the information around the network and, together with the network operating system, performs a number of functions including:

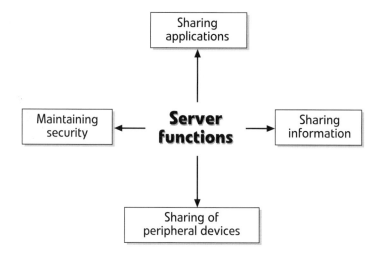

Applications and data can be managed more effectively when they are managed by a server. Auditing functions can also be undertaken more easily to ensure that data is kept secure.

Within larger networks there may be servers that are dedicated to a specific resource or function, for example:

- print servers
- file servers
- mail servers
- servers that are reserved for data storage.

Test your knowledge

1 Identify the benefits that a networked system can bring to an organisation.
2 Network structures can be described as being LANs, MANs, WANs and VANs. Compare and contrast each of these structures in terms of their capabilities and their benefits to an organisation.
3 State two advantages and two disadvantages of a distributed database.
4 Outline the differences between a homogenous and a heterogeneous distributed database system.
5 Define the key components in a client/server system and give examples of different server types.

Exam questions

1 As an ICT manager in a medium-sized company, you have been asked to create a job specification for a database administrator.

(a) Describe **three** responsibilities you would include in this specification. *(6 marks)*
(b) The database that this person will be in charge of is a client/server database. Describe **two** advantages of using this type of database over a non-client/server database. *(4 marks)*

AQA June 2002

5 Network security, audit and accounting

Although networks can bring many benefits to an organisation, there are also some drawbacks to having a networked environment. One of the major drawbacks is caused by the 'shared' element of network use, and the increased security risks.

The security risks can be categorised into:

- unauthorised access by internal users
- external threats: vandalism, theft and sabotage.

Keeping data secure on a network can be difficult because of the environment in which users work and the access they require to data. With the movement towards a totally networked environment promoting a culture of 'sharing', the issue of data security is even more important and needs to be addressed at a number of levels. Measures that can be taken to protect network traffic against illegal access and other security threats, are shown in Figure 6.

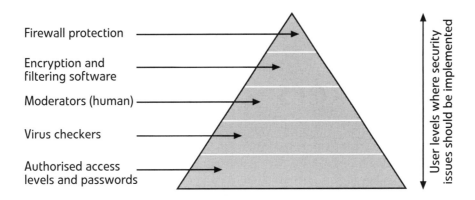

Figure 6

Levels of security

5.0 Firewall protection

The primary aim of a firewall is to guard against unauthorised access to an internal network. In effect, a firewall is a gateway with a lock – the gateway opens only for information packets that pass one or more security inspections.

There are three basic types of firewalls.

- **Application gateways** – the first gateways, sometimes referred to as proxy gateways. These are made up of hosts that run special software to act as a proxy server. Clients behind the firewall must know how to use the proxy, and be configured to do so in order to use Internet services.
- **Packet filtering** – a technique whereby routers have 'access control lists' turned on. By default, a router will pass all traffic sent without any restrictions. Because packet filtering is done with routers, it is often much faster than application gateways.

■ **Hybrid system** – a mixture of application gateways and packet filtering. In some of these systems, new connections must be authenticated and approved at the application layer. Once this has been done, the remainder of the connection is passed to the session layer, where packet filters watch the connection to ensure that only packets that are part of an ongoing (already authenticated and approved) conversation are being passed.

5.1 Encryption and filtering software

Encryption software scrambles message transmissions. When a message is encrypted a secret numerical code or **encryption key** is applied, and the message can be transmitted or stored in indecipherable characters. The message can be read only after it has been reconstructed through the use of a **matching key**.

5.2 Moderators

Moderators are people who have the responsibility of controlling, filtering and restricting the information that is shared across a network within an organisation.

5.3 Virus checkers

Virus checkers are programs designed to search for viruses, notify users of their existence and remove them from infected files or disks.

5.4 Authorised access levels and passwords

On a networked system, various privilege levels can be set up to restrict user access to shared resources such as files, folders, printers and other peripheral devices. A password system can also be implemented to divide levels of entry according to job role and information requirements.

For example, a finance assistant may need access to personnel data when generating the monthly payroll. Data about employees may, however, be password protected in the human resources department – so special permissions may be required to gain access to this data.

5.5 Audit control software

This will allow an organisation to monitor and record what is on its network at any point in time, and provide an opportunity to check that what is on the system has been authorised and is legal.

Over a period of time a number of factors could impact upon how much software an organisation acquires without its knowledge. These can include:

- illegal copying of software by employees
- downloading of software by employees
- installation of software by employees
- exceeding licenced use of software.

These interventions by employees may occur with little or no consideration of the organisation's responsibility to ensure that software is not misused or abused.

5.6 Data quality audit

In conjunction with audits on software, audits can also be carried out to identify and correct faulty data. A data quality audit is a structured survey of the accuracy and level of completeness of data in an information system. This type of audit can be carried out using the following methods:

- surveying end users to gather their perceptions on data quality
- surveying samples gathered from data files
- surveying entire data files.

Audit trails can be used for a number of reasons, including checking files to see what information has been changed or updated, when and by whom. Audit trails are also written into applications and recorded with each transaction.

Unless regular data quality audits are undertaken, organisations have no way of knowing to what extent their networked system contains inaccurate, incomplete or ambiguous information. The complexity of individual systems in an organisation – such as stock control, ordering or payroll – and the networking of data could mean that an error in one data set on a system could be distributed among other systems. This could cause major inaccuracies that may lie undiscovered for days, months or even years.

5.7 Importance of network security

Network security is a crucial factor for an organisation, especially with the growth in trade and business via e-commerce. Systems that provide secure transactions are vital to organisations, ensuring that customers and suppliers feel confident that any payments and other details remain confidential.

One company that has succeeded in providing network security assurance is VeriSign.

Case study

Solutions | Products & Services | Support | About VeriSign | Contact | Search | ›› |

INTELLIGENCE AND CONTROL SERVICES

Network Security

UNITED STATES

SECURITY & PAYMENT SERVICES»

Network Security

Managed Security Services

Network Security Consulting

Resources

Guides and Trials

White Papers

Data Sheets

Success Stories

Events

Traditional enterprise network boundaries are dissolving rapidly as businesses expand globally and open up their networks and applications to partners and mobile employees. Simultaneously, technologies such as Wireless LANs are adding an additional layer of complexity to network security.

VeriSign is in a unique position to help enterprises design and deploy cost-effective, scalable network security solutions. VeriSign operates critical Internet infrastructure services such as the DNS root server infrastructure, which handles over 10 billion lookups a day. As a result, VeriSign has unique data and intelligence about network security patterns and trends, which are used to identify and respond to potential security threats proactively and effectively.

VeriSign Network Security helps customers leverage Intelligence and Control^{SM} to gain better control and efficiency over their security environments.

Broadband

⇨ Watch the Network Security Seminar

Documentation

White Papers

» Internet Security Intelligence Briefing

» MSS: Securing Your Critical Networks

» Understanding Network Vulnerabilities

» Enterprise Security: Changing Needs, Evolving Response

» Securing Wireless Local Area Networks

▣ Intelligence and Control Services: The New Age of Information Security

---

VeriSign is used by a multitude of organisations both large and small, for its ability to provide tailored network security solutions, as can be seen in its portfolio of customer profiles, examples of which include:

- Merrill Lynch
- Powergen
- US Securities and Exchange Commerce
- Ernst and Young.

VeriSign
The Value of Trust™

Customer Profile

Solution Summary

Industry
Human Resources

Challenge
To create a secure system for managing employee benefits for over 3,000 organizations.

Solution
VeriSign Managed PKI for SSL, and VeriSign Security Consulting.

Results
- Better brand recognition with the increased level of security
- With the security structures in place, the company was able to develop into a solid, more well-organized business
- The security measures require very little maintenance

Morneau Sobeco is one of the many organisations that have turned to VeriSign for a network security solution. Morneau Sobeco, a human resource organisation, required a secure system for managing employee benefits. Verisign supplied the solution:

W.F. Morneau & Associates was founded in 1966 and developed a reputation for benefits consulting and administration. Sobeco, founded in 1962, specialised in pension design, consulting, and administration. Morneau Sobeco was founded in 1997 when the two firms joined. Prior to the growth of the Web in the early nineties, Morneau Sobeco used paper- and fax-based systems. Currently, the company uses highly comprehensive network, three telephone call centres, and systems that can be securely and easily accessed via the Web. Morneau Sobeco builds back-end services that clients transparently deploy on their own sites. From offices distributed across twelve North American cities, Morneau Sobeco serves more than 3,000 clients that include corporations, professional associations, charitable organisations, and trade associations.

Providing Security With VeriSign

With so many companies accessing Morneau Sobeco's systems, and because the data is of a highly sensitive nature, the company couldn't afford to take chances when it came to security. Just as Fortune 500 organisations turn to Morneau Sobeco for benefits management, Morneau Sobeco turned to VeriSign to ensure that the right users gained access to the right information. 'In this economy, our customers are looking at all ways to save money,' explains Allen Gates, Director of Systems Infrastructure. 'Outsourcing critical services that aren't core to a company's business saves a ton of money. That's smart business.' Morneau Sobeco used VeriSign's Managed PKI for SSL to allow the company to easily and safely distribute certificates for secure identification and authorisation. Before Morneau Sobeco used MPKI, it took several days to acquire a certificate, but now, the company can obtain a certificate in just a few hours. 'We're getting the services we expect and we're very happy,' says Gates. 'MPKI works extremely well – it saves time so it's much more efficient.' Morneau Sobeco's clients had been consistently asking for SSL Secure Site certification, and Gates was glad to be able to provide it. 'The Secure Site seal is like a check box for our customers,' Gates says. 'The VeriSign name adds credibility and satisfies that check box.'

Testing the Foundations

Morneau Sobeco was confident in the security of its network and application environment. However, the company was looking for a third party penetration test and report on the systems that could be used to address any oversights and validate a strong security posture to investors, business partners, and potential clients. Once again, Morneau Sobeco turned to VeriSign to conduct a focused penetration effort on specific, external segments of the company's network. VeriSign followed its standard penetration test methodology of Profile, Scan, Enumerate, Exploit, Report, and Present. The objective of the testing was to measure the degree of network and application visibility available to unauthorised users attempting to access the systems over the Internet. VeriSign produced two versions of its final deliverable. One version was used internally by Morneau Sobeco to support issue remediation and another version was created as an external security validation document to be shared with business partners, investors, and clients. 'The VeriSign team was very professional,' says Gates. 'They developed documents that were well put together and very helpful. We used them internally and distributed them to our customers upon request. Our customers know VeriSign; the brand validates us in our customers' eyes.'

1 Why did Morneau Sobeco turn to Verisign?

2 What difference did the use of Secure Site certification make to the organisation and its customers? Why was it important to have the VeriSign name?

3 What is VeriSign's 'standard penetration test methodology' and in what context has this been used for Morneau Sobeco?

Test your knowledge

1 What security risks exist on a networked system, and what measures can be taken to address these?

2 There are three different types of firewall:
- application gateways
- packet filtering
- hybrid systems.

Explain what each firewall type is and how it works.

3 What is the purpose of audit control software?

4 What is meant by a *data quality audit*?

 Exam questions

1 **(a)** Describe **two** changes that may be evident to end users when they change over from using a stand-alone computer to a networked environment. *(4 marks)*

   (b) A multinational company has recently created an Intranet, connecting all of its computer systems. All its sites are now connected using high-speed dedicated links.

   (i) Describe **one** facility that could now be made available to the company which would improve productivity. *(2 marks)*

   (ii) Describe **two** possible problems that may arise as a result of using this network of computer systems. *(4 marks)*

   (iii) Describe **two** possible measures that the company can take to combat problems caused by the use of this type of network. *(4 marks)*

   AQA June 2002

2 Whilst planning to install a network accounting system, a company has become concerned about the security of its local computer network.

   (a) Explain **two** procedures that the company could adopt to discourage breaches of security. *(6 marks)*

   (b) State **two** reasons for using accounting software on a network. *(2 marks)*

   AQA Jan 2003

6 Human/computer interaction

Human/computer interaction involves the study of methods for designing the input and output screens for a given system, to ensure that it is user friendly. The main factors that should be taken into consideration in human/computer interaction design can be seen in Figure 7.

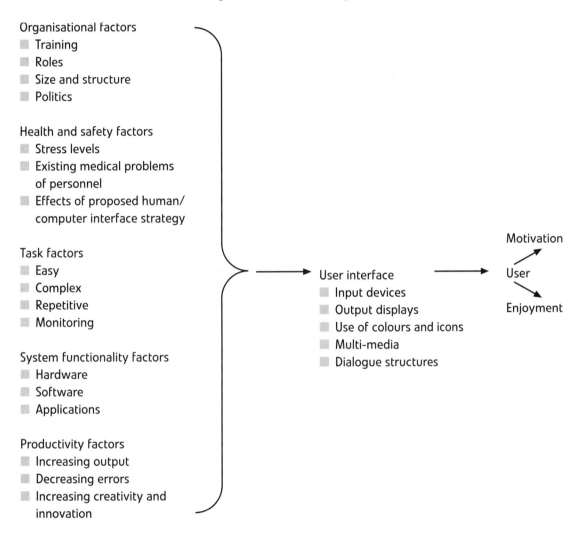

Organisational factors
- Training
- Roles
- Size and structure
- Politics

Health and safety factors
- Stress levels
- Existing medical problems of personnel
- Effects of proposed human/ computer interface strategy

Task factors
- Easy
- Complex
- Repetitive
- Monitoring

System functionality factors
- Hardware
- Software
- Applications

Productivity factors
- Increasing output
- Decreasing errors
- Increasing creativity and innovation

User interface
- Input devices
- Output displays
- Use of colours and icons
- Multi-media
- Dialogue structures

Motivation

User

Enjoyment

Figure 7

Factors in human/computer interaction design

The way in which users interact with computers depends on a range of factors, as shown in Figure 7. Other factors that need to be taken into consideration are the human elements of cognition and perception, motor performance, personality and culture.

Therefore design should take into account an end user's:

- memory (short-, medium- and long-term) and learning
- problem-solving and decision-making abilities
- attention span, perception and recognition
- anxieties and fears

- age and gender
- response to stimuli
- vision
- hearing
- touch and co-ordination
- physical strength
- personality
- disabilities
- awareness of culture and international diversity (customs, etiquette, formalities and tradition).

Certain measures can be taken to address each of these. In terms of the psychological factors, a system can be designed that:

- is user friendly
- provides support and help to novice users
- provides short cuts for more advanced or expert users
- makes use of human long-term memory to maximise efficiency.

Users are of different types, and the profile of each user type has an impact on the type of interface that needs to be designed for them. For example, a novice user will not be familiar with the layout or functions of a particular interface, therefore any interface would need to be simple, clear, instructive and possibly graphical.

Examples of interface tools designed for novice/first-time users are shown in Figure 8.

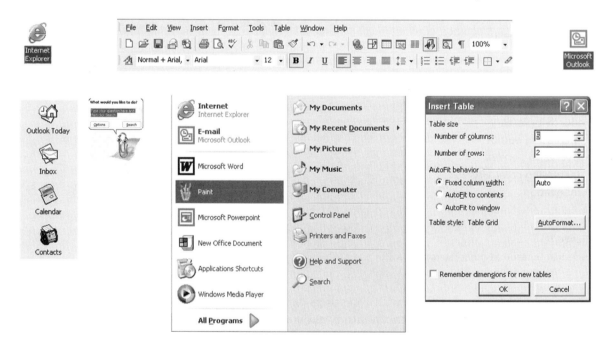

Figure 8
Interface tools designed for novice users

Some organisations, such as IBM and Microsoft, provide specific solutions for software taking into account its ease of use, realising that systems should be user-driven as well as functionally driven – see Figure 9.

Ease of Use

 Attribute Explorer

rapid data analysis through attribute bar chats

 NotesBuddy

e-mail and instant messenger

 Systems Journal

featuring ease of use topics

Ease of use is vital to the success of most products and services. The user experience directly affects sales, service cost, productive use, customer loyalty and almost every other aspect of doing business. In the following seven sections, this site addresses the challenge of creating great user experiences through the discipline of User Engineering, supported by design guidelines, tools, services and other relevant materials.

Value

Discover a compelling value proposition for improving your total user experience.

User Engineering

Learn about the definitive process for designing user experiences that satisfy and exceed user expectations.

Services

Find out how IBM's experienced professionals can assist you in designing outstanding products and solutions.

Downloads

Try out the various applications, resources and UCD tools that will help improve usability.

Journal

Get the latest information on ease of use from IBM and featured companies. Subscribe to the monthly newsletter.

Design

Explore design principles and guidelines for Web sites, desktops, 'out-of-box' and other common experiences.

Conference

The annual Make IT Easy conference is a forum for the exchange of ideas and information on ease of use with IT professionals from around the world.

Reproduced by permission from IBM © 2004 by International Business Machines Corporation

Figure 9

IBM's solutions for usability

Test your knowledge

1 Explain what is meant by the term *human/computer interaction*.
2 What design factors should be taken into consideration in terms of human/computer interaction?
3 What psychological factors could affect human/computer interaction, and what steps can be taken to address and overcome these?
4 In what ways do different users impact upon interface design?
5 What interface issues should be taken into consideration for expert users?

Exam questions

1 **(a)** Describe **two** factors that need to be considered when designing for human/computer interaction. *(4 marks)*

(b) Describe **two** resource implications of providing an effective interface. *(4 marks)*

(c) Some users may customise their interface.

Describe **one** consequence this may have for support staff when providing technical assistance. *(2 marks)*

AQA June 2002

7 Human/computer interface (HCI)

For an organisation, the question of how users can work with ICT systems confidently and positively has many resource implications.

If software is designed without reference to how end users will interact with it, the consequences are far-reaching. If users are unable to interact effectively with the software, this could result in:

- low or no productivity
- delay in fulfilling task requirements
- resentment towards software use
- refusal to undertake tasks that are software driven
- the need for further training and frequent re-training.

Software development has a life-cycle, and one of the most important aspects of this life-cycle is the interface design. The issues related to the human/computer interface focus on user-centred design as opposed to systems-centred design.

What does this mean?	
User-centred design:	Design centred on a user's needs and working environment.
System-centred design:	Design built around the system, addressing issues such as: 'what can be built easily on this platform?'

User-centred design takes into account a user's:

- working environment
- job roles and tasks
- abilities, needs and requirements.

The process of design is a collaboration between the end user and the programmers/designers, to ensure that the user can interact effectively with the software and system.

A user-centred design approach can have the following implications for an organisation.

- Costs may be increased as more user-friendly adjustments and customisations may have to be built into any software that is designed – especially more specialist software.
- The development and implementation process may take longer as end users would have input into the overall design.
- There may be a conflict of interest between what end users want and what programmers want to develop.
- Issues of ownership may arise – if end users have contributed to the development, they may resent any future changes being made.

Software can be customised to develop a specialist HCI through the use of specialised tools known as **interface tools** and **visual development tools**. These tools can focus specifically on the different stages of software development and they allow rapid graphical user interface development.

Examples of these tools include:

- Microsoft Visual Basic
- Delphi
- Toolbook
- Java.

These tools provide interface capabilities such as 'drag and drop' buttons, fields and combo boxes.

It is evident that there needs to be a careful balance between functionality and the issue of HCI in software development and design.

Any interface design should take into account the level of user, as shown in the table below.

User interface design profiles	
User type	**Interface type**
Novice/first time: assume that this user type has minimal knowledge of both task and interface	■ Simple ■ Easily accessed ■ Built-in help, and tutorial facilities ■ Graphical ■ Drag and drop commands
Knowledgeable/intermittent user: some knowledge, but may have a problem remembering functions and commands	■ Emphasis on recognition ■ Consistency ■ Context-sensitive (to fill in knowledge gaps)
Expert/frequent user: familiar with task and interface, needs minimal prompts and reminders	■ Fast response ■ Short-cuts available ■ Textual

Although the range of hardware and software available to support PCs, Macs, Linux, Unix and other operating systems is quite diverse, the interfaces are very similar. Interfaces across this range have evolved from text-based DOS-type systems – UNIX or graphical Windows type systems, and Linux and Macintosh with menu- and icon-driven screens.

However, some new advances in interfaces and tools to support HCI have been made, especially with the emergence of good mobile phone technology. Features such as colour screens, voice recognition dialling and predictive texting have aided users of all levels.

Case study

The need for a useable software interface is outlined in an article in *Computer Weekly*. The article outlines the importance to end users and an organisation of designing and making the right software choice.

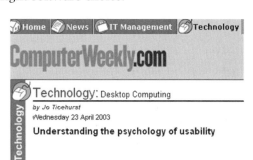

No matter how well an IT system runs, if the user interface is wrong productivity will suffer. It is up to IT managers to put themselves in the users' shoes.

Many instruction leaflets supplied with flat-pack furniture can be nigh on impossible to follow. Why can't manufacturers make such products as simple to assemble and use as a child's toy?

The same can be true of software. As IT systems become increasingly complex, the learning curve for users is getting steeper. In some cases, making the right software choice can mean the difference between success and failure. There are many facets to user interface design that IT departments must consider before deciding what software to use. A well-designed, intuitive IT system means less training and support for end-users.

It is important that IT staff understand the end-user experience. 'You should put yourself in the position of your users,' said Robina Chatham, visiting fellow at the Cranfield School of Management. She warned that many IT professionals are drawn to technically challenging areas of functionality, but this does not necessarily produce easy-to-use software. 'Consider what your users really need rather than the features of the software. How much do they actually use?'

User-friendly interfaces

In any software, whether commercial or bespoke, giving the end-user too many options is confusing. 'If it is too complicated, many users will just give up.'

Brian Oakley, an expert on the subject of usability at the British Computer Society's Human-Computer Interface Specialist Group, agreed. 'Remember that the person is at the heart of the system. Many systems have gone wrong because people become enthralled by technology.' Oakley warned that most users hate delays. 'Three seconds is manageable, but when a system begins to take more than 20 seconds, users start doing something else,' he said.

Productivity is also affected if a system is too complex, or if end users have been given inadequate training in how to use the software. Even something as simple as the colours used on your company's systems can affect how people work. 'People do not like to be bombarded with bright colours – their eyes can get very tired,' said Oakley.

He said application developers should avoid using garish hues such as bright reds and yellows and keep the number of colours to a minimum. Choose muted pastel shades such as green and blue when designing user interfaces, he said. Dresner feels that fantastically designed GUIs are not what users need if they are required to work in a particular way. He suggests designing the interface so that it is fit for purpose and satisfying to use. 'Think about the information the user will need on the screen,' he said.

So what exactly makes the definitive user interface? Microsoft is one company whose balance sheet relies on knowing what users want. It claims to have spent more than $3bn (£1.9bn) on the research and development of its Office productivity suite to build the most intuitive user experience in the product range.

One result of this research was a subtle change in screen colours. Daniel Bennie, Microsoft Office product marketing manager, said the research showed that users wanted text that was easier to read on screen. The result was that Microsoft introduced a grey border around e-mail messages in Outlook to make the message appear more prominent.

Besides colour changes, the formatting of text can have a huge impact on usability. Bennie said, 'We have also included a feature that enables users to read the text in columns like they would read a newspaper, as this is easier for the eye to scan.'

1 What are the key elements that IT staff and professionals should consider when developing software?

2 What does Brian Oakley warn in regard to system delays? Do you agree?

3 One comment in the article is that you should 'think about the information the user will need on the screen'. Why is this important?

Test your knowledge

1   What are the implications of designing software without reference to how end users will interact?

2   Describe the concept of user-centred design.

3   There are a number of implications for an organisation adopting a user-centred design approach – evaluate two of these.

4   What are the reasons why a systems-centred design may be produced?

Exam questions

1   A mail order music company has decided to expand and has established a retail outlet in a busy shopping centre.

(a) An important feature of the mail-order system is the interface for the staff who use it. State **three** features you would expect the human/computer interface to have in such a system and give a different reason for each one.   *(6 marks)*

(b) (i) Name an appropriate device for capturing data on each item that is sold via the retail outlet.   *(1 mark)*

(ii) Describe **one** advantage for the company of using this device.   *(2 marks)*

AQA Jan 2003

8 Software development

There are a number of methods that can be used to develop software solutions. These include:

- user-written solutions

- internal development by a team or department

- using a software house to develop generic or bespoke software solutions.

8.0 Internal development

Internally, software solutions can be devised at an individual, group or corporate level, as shown in Figure 10.

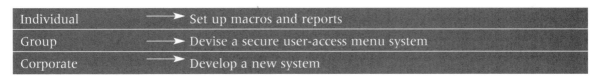

Individual	⟶	Set up macros and reports
Group	⟶	Devise a secure user-access menu system
Corporate	⟶	Develop a new system

Figure 10

Examples of internal software solutions

User-written solutions can be tailored to a specific task requirement; for example, a user might generate a report on a database application as a solution to consolidating information on all customers who live within a specific postcode area.

A group of people within a department may devise a security system giving access rights to certain users on a system. By setting up passwords as a solution, they could restrict users to certain levels depending upon their job role. For example, an accounts manager may have access to all information, whereas an accounts clerk may be restricted to the payroll.

At a corporate level, software solutions may be developed to meet the functional needs of a number of departments or for an entire branch. In-house developers may design or revise a payroll, customer accounts or ordering system.

One of the benefits of developing software in-house is the cost. If a company is using the expertise of staff members, the cost of developing software solutions may be greatly reduced in comparison with outsourcing to a software house.

8.1 Software houses

For organisations that do not have the expertise, time or resources to develop software solutions in-house, there is the option of using a software house.

Software houses can provide tailor-made solutions through the use of specialist or bespoke software, or an off-the-shelf solution using a standard application.

An example of this is Microsoft Business Solutions, as shown in Figure 11. This provides a portfolio of software solutions including:

- Axapta
- Navision
- Soloman.
- Great Plains
- Microsoft CRM

These solutions are suitable for a range of businesses including charities, public sector organisations, healthcare, retail, IT, financial services, travel and leisure companies and more.

Microsoft *Business Solutions*

See how our customers are benefiting from our solutions

Microsoft® Business Solutions Products and Services are delivered almost exclusively by our network of Partners – specialists who understand your business and your industry in depth, and can help you maximise the effectiveness of your systems.

Our global network of 4,500 Partners provides a local personalised service and they are specialists to a wide range of industries including the public sector industry.

Figure 11

Microsoft business solutions

In order to build a suitable solution and provide an instant personalised recommendation, Microsoft has an on-line feature that allows organisations to input details about their needs and requirements, as shown in Figure 12.

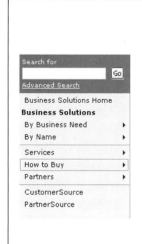

Microsoft Business Solutions

Business Solutions Home | Solution Builder | Business Solutions Worldwide

Build a Solution

To help find the right solution for your business, tell us a little about your needs below. Your answers will be used to display an instant personalised solution recommendation, listing specific products you'll want to learn more about. If you're not sure what a particular question or option means, choose 'Learn More' or click the underlined words to get a definition.

Currently, most solutions recommended with this tool focus on North America business needs, although many are available in multiple countries. If your business is based outside of the U.S. or Canada – or if you require multinational capabilities – contact the Microsoft Business Solutions office in your region to learn more about the right solution for your business. All budget ranges stated in the recommendations are in US dollars.

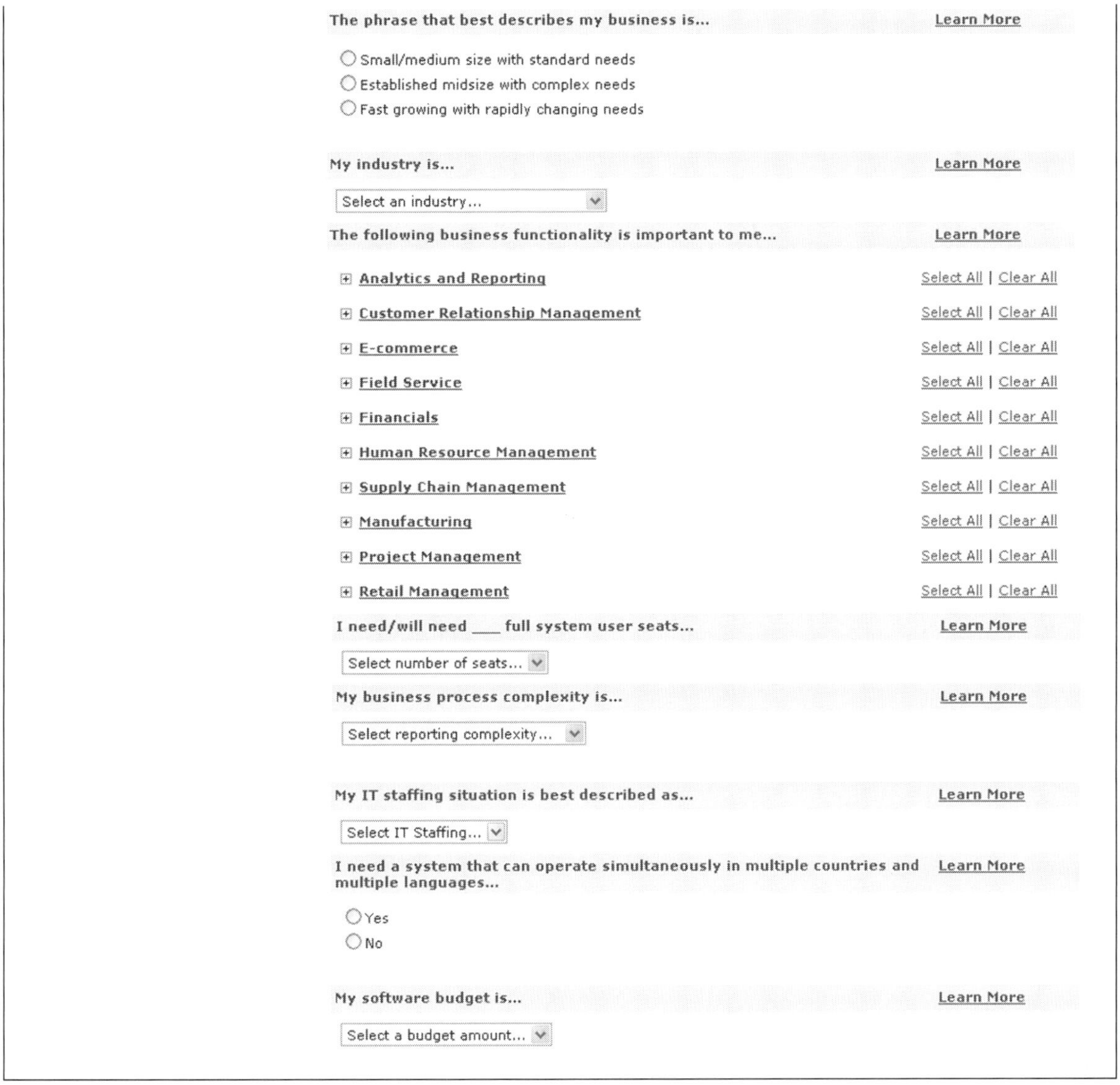

The phrase that best describes my business is...   Learn More

   ○ Small/medium size with standard needs
   ○ Established midsize with complex needs
   ○ Fast growing with rapidly changing needs

My industry is...   Learn More

   [Select an industry...   ▼]

The following business functionality is important to me...   Learn More

   ⊞ **Analytics and Reporting**   Select All | Clear All

   ⊞ **Customer Relationship Management**   Select All | Clear All

   ⊞ **E-commerce**   Select All | Clear All

   ⊞ **Field Service**   Select All | Clear All

   ⊞ **Financials**   Select All | Clear All

   ⊞ **Human Resource Management**   Select All | Clear All

   ⊞ **Supply Chain Management**   Select All | Clear All

   ⊞ **Manufacturing**   Select All | Clear All

   ⊞ **Project Management**   Select All | Clear All

   ⊞ **Retail Management**   Select All | Clear All

I need/will need ____ full system user seats...   Learn More

   [Select number of seats... ▼]

My business process complexity is...   Learn More

   [Select reporting complexity... ▼]

My IT staffing situation is best described as...   Learn More

   [Select IT Staffing... ▼]

I need a system that can operate simultaneously in multiple countries and   Learn More
multiple languages...

   ○ Yes
   ○ No

My software budget is...   Learn More

   [Select a budget amount... ▼]

Figure 12

On-line solutions

Test your knowledge

1   In what different ways can software solutions be provided? Compare and contrast these ways at different organisational levels.
2   Software acquisition and solutions can form part of an organisation's corporate strategy. Identify the key elements to such a strategy.

Exam questions

1 A software company is producing a software package to perform an initial assessment of students entering colleges.

(a) There is a fixed deadline for the release of this package.
Describe **two** effects that this might have on the final product. *(4 marks)*

(b) The production of this package is a complex task. For this reason the company has decided to allocate sub-tasks to separate development teams.
Describe **two** benefits of this approach. *(4 marks)*

(c) Two weeks after the release of the package, several colleges report identical problems with the software.
Describe what the company should do in this situation *(2 marks)*

AQA Jan 2003

2 Software solutions can be provided for specialist applications in a number of ways.
Discuss the possible ways of providing such solutions. Your discussion should include:

- how the solution can be provided
- advantages of providing the solution in this way
- disadvantages of providing the solution in this way
- criteria for deciding which approach is the most appropriate. *(20 marks)*

AQA Jan 2003

9 Software reliability

9.0 Testing software

Testing is vital to the successful development and implementation of software. The stages of software testing will vary depending on which phase is being addressed. For example, during the prototyping phase, testing may be more ad hoc as the aim is to identify any features that are missing or to define different ways of performing a task or function. During the implementation phase, however, testing becomes more structured in order to identify as many faults as possible.

Throughout the software life-cycle, a testing model can be applied. This identifies the various aspects of testing through analysis and design to testing against the requirements specification (user acceptance test), and the detailed design (unit testing). This model is known as the V-model, and is illustrated in Figure 13.

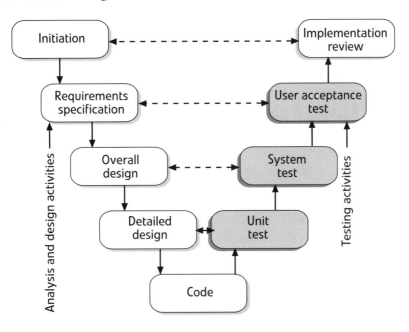

Figure 13

V-model of testing in relation to analysis and design

Testing can be broken down into a number of levels and stages, structured in the form of a hierarchy, as shown in Figure 14.

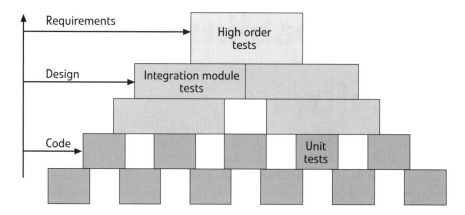

Figure 14

Testing hierarchy

Although software may go through a number of testing stages, it may still fail to work or initiate successfully when implemented as part of an IT system. The reasons for this can include:

- incompatibility of coding, programs and data across platforms
- level and expertise of the end-user
- problems with the systems hardware – not fast enough, inadequate memory, etc.

9.1 High-order tests

High-order testing can be broken down into a number of areas. These include:

- validation tests (alpha and beta test)
- system tests
- other specialised tests (performance, security, etc.).

Alpha and beta tests take place before packaged software is released. The purpose of **alpha tests** is to identify any bugs or major problems that may affect software functionality or usability in the early build phase. This type of testing is usually carried out in-house by staff members.

Beta tests occur after the alpha tests to identify any bugs in the software before it is released to customers.

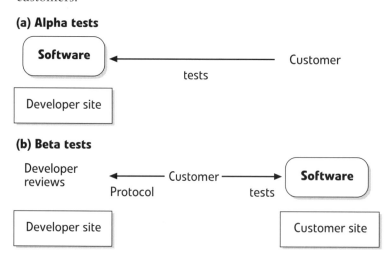

Figure 15

Overview of alpha and beta tests

Case study

An example of beta testing can be seen in the article below from *Computer Weekly*.

The company released the advance copy of XP SP2 to give IT professionals a chance to test and give feedback on latest features and configuration changes in SP2. Many of those changes were introduced to make computers running XP less susceptible to viruses and worms, such as the recent Blaster.

Microsoft called the XP SP2 beta version release a 'milestone' in its effort to make XP and its customers more secure. The features released this week are a 'subset' of those that will be included in the final release of SP2. Beta testers' feedback will help Microsoft determine which features to include and omit. (www.microsoft.com/presspass/newsroom/winxp/WindowsXPSPFS.asp.)

Among the changes in the operating system is an improved version of firewall software that ships with XP. Formerly known as the Internet Connection Firewall, that software is now called the Windows Firewall and is turned on by default, blocking Windows communications ports that are not being used by software applications installed on an XP machine.

Beta testing will ensure the Windows Firewall does not disrupt software applications running on Windows when SP2 ships to customers, Microsoft said.

Microsoft also turned off a controversial administrative tool called Windows Messenger service, which allowed computers on a network to display text messages in pop-up desktop windows. That feature had been discovered by spammers and used to display advertisements and had recently been the subject of a critical security patch from Microsoft.

Other security changes in XP SP2 are more subtle.

Microsoft changed Windows implementation of RPC (Remote Procedure Call) that will make it harder for attackers to exploit that service. Recent worms such as Blaster and Nachi used a security vulnerability in RPC to infect Windows machines.

The company also locked down the Component Object Model (Com) that governs the way software applications run in the Windows environment and exchange information over a computer network. Security holes in a component of Com called the Distributed Component Object Model (DCom) were behind the Blaster and Nachi internet worms earlier this year.

Changes in the software used to compile Windows XP's underlying computer code has also made the operating system less vulnerable to buffer overrun attacks, which are flaws in underlying software code that can allow hackers to crash Windows or take control of vulnerable systems.

On the application front, Microsoft has changed the Internet Explorer web browser, Outlook Express e-mail client and Windows Messenger instant messaging program, making it harder to use those programs for launching malicious programs disguised as web page downloads or e-mail and IM file attachments.

Windows XP SP2 also contains a host of other enhancements, including improvements to the Automatic Update feature so that updates are easier for users with low-capacity dial-up connections to download and install.

Other improvements include a new version of Windows Media Player, better support for wireless hotspots and wireless devices such as keyboards, wireless printers and PDA using the Bluetooth wireless technology.

Feedback from developers on the beta version of XP SP2 will be used to improve the final version of the product, due in the first half of 2004.

Paul Roberts writes for IDG News Service

1 What changes did Microsoft make to this latest release?

2 Why were these changes required?

3 What is meant by RPC, and what have Microsoft done to make this more secure?

9.2 **Unit tests**

Integration and module tests can be one of a number of different types, including:

- big bang
- top-down
- bottom-up
- regression testing.

The unit testing environment is shown in Figure 16. Unit testing tests individual modules to ensure that they function correctly for any given inputs.

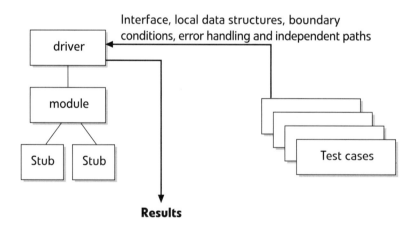

Figure 16

Unit testing environment

9.3 Maintenance release

A maintenance release is issued when a newer, more updated version of a product is available. The newer version may include a range of additional features or amendments that can:

- meet the changing needs and demands of customers
- address problems in a previous version
- update certain tools or programs to make it more functional, user friendly, secure or compatible.

Most maintenance releases are an enhancement to an existing version of a product, as opposed to a complete replacement, as in the case study below.

Case study

Press release

Microsoft Windows Small Business Server 2003 Released to Manufacturing

Final Release in Windows Server 2003 Family Tailored To Meet Specific Needs of Small Businesses

Reading – UK – September 16th 2002 – Microsoft Ltd today announced that Windows Small Business Server 2003 has been released to manufacturing. Based on groundbreaking innovations that dramatically simplify the deployment process, ongoing management and use of server technology, Windows Small Business Server 2003 enables small-business customers to ensure that their data is automatically protected, significantly increase their productivity and improve their connection with customers. Specifically tailored to address the requirements of small businesses, Windows Small Business Server 2003 now makes server technology a viable and approachable option for this under-served market segment.

Windows Small Business Server 2003 enables small-business technology providers to expand their customer base and services portfolio by offering a server technology solution that can be quickly and easily deployed, managed and used. With Windows Small Business Server 2003, partners benefit from the product's integration because they spend less time on technology implementation and maintenance and can focus more on higher-value services and offerings for their customers.

1. What is the function of and market for Windows Small Business Server 2003?
2. What enhancements have been provided in this maintenance release?

Test your knowledge

1. Why is software testing so important?
2. Compare and contrast the features and characteristics of alpha and beta testing.
3. What is meant by the term *maintenance release*? Research two other examples of this.

Exam questions

1. Software houses go through a long testing programme before releasing a product. Despite this, problems can still occur with that product.
   Give **three** reasons why testing may not be completely successful. *(3 marks)*

   AQA June 2002

10 Portability of data

The ability to transfer data across different software types, applications, systems and platforms is essential in today's dynamic environment, which is driven by IT communications. However, the diversity of hardware and software available and increasing file sizes can make portability quite difficult.

There are a number of ways to ensure that data can be transferred more easily across applications and platforms. These include:

- reducing or compressing file sizes (through the use of tools such as PKZip, Winzip and FreeZip)
- using customised tools such as 'pack and go' in presentation software
- transferring a file type from Bitmap to GIF (so that as opposed to being saved bit by bit, repetitive information is removed).

Software companies such as Microsoft will always provide users with options to save information in an older format, for example saving files in Office 98 format when using Office XP, or to ensure compatibility with other applications, as shown in Figure 17.

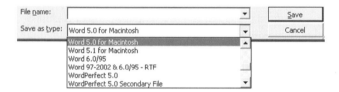

Figure 17
File types

10.0 Protocols and standards

A protocol can be defined as the method of communication used between network components that form part of a standard. It is the pre-defined way that someone who wants to use a service communicates with that service. This could be a person, but more often it is a computer program like a Web browser.

Protocols include:

- transmission control protocol (TCP) and Internet protocol (IP) – for passing data packets around the Internet
- HTTP – used to allow computers to transfer and process HTML files
- SMTP – mail protocol that allows e-mail to be sent across the Internet
- FTP – allowing files to be uploaded and downloaded.

Transmission control protocol (TCP) and Internet protocol (IP) were developed to connect a number of different networks designed by different vendors into a network of networks – the Internet.

TCP/IP is composed of a number of layers:

- IP moves the packet of data from node to node – forwarding each packet based on its address

- TCP is responsible for verifying the correct delivery of data from client to server
- Sockets: a package of sub-routines that provides access to TCP/IP on the majority of systems.

IP is the language that computers use to communicate over the Internet. Every machine on the Internet has a IP address. A typical IP address looks like this:

196.168.0.X

The four numbers in an IP address are called octets, because they each have eight positions when viewed in binary form. Octets are used to create classes of IP addresses that can be assigned to a particular business, government or other entity based on size and need. Octets are split into two sections:

- net
- host.

The **net** section always contains the first octet. It is used to identify the network that a computer belongs to. The **host** always contains the last octet and identifies the actual computer on the network.

10.1 Emergence of standards

Where do standards come from?

De facto standards are those that have become a standard because they have been widely used and recognised by the industry.

Some examples of de facto standards include:

- Hayes command set for controlling modems
- Xmodem Communications Protocol
- Hewlett-Packard Printer Control Language (PCL) for laser printers.

Marketplace forces lead to de facto standards. They are imposed by dominant vendors within a market. Such standards are missing on the Web today, but there are clearly leading companies, such as Amazon.com, whose designs are widely copied.

Standardisation on the Web mirrors the benefits that interface standards have provided in the world of desktop software, in terms of lower development costs and higher usability. Development costs are lower because there are fewer unique design decisions to be made. For routine design decisions, designers can rely on standards published by platform vendors (such as Apple's Aqua Human Interface Guidelines and Microsoft's Windows User Experience).

Partially standardised applications on a given platform are more usable because users can transfer part of what they know about one application to the use of another application.

Test your knowledge

1 How can data be transferred more easily across different applications and platforms?
2 What is meant by a de facto standard? Give an example of this type.
3 What is an Internet protocol?

Exam question

1 Describe **two** distinct ways in which standards can arise within the ICT industry. *(4 marks)*

AQA Jan 2003

2 Networks of computers are rapidly becoming part of everyday life, both for organisations and individuals. Communication over networks involves the use of prototcols.

(a) Define the term *protocol*. *(1 mark)*

(b) With the aid of an example, describe one advantage of using protocols. *(3 marks)*

(c) State **one** consideration that should be taken into account when setting up a network, and explain why it is important. *(2 marks)*

AQA June 2002

UNIT 6 – COURSEWORK:
USE OF INFORMATION SYSTEMS FOR PROBLEM SOLVING

This unit will help to support you in the selection, development, design and implementation of a suitable project using generic application software.

It is divided into a number of key sections, covering:

- Project considerations
- Process skills – review of applications software packages
- Analysis
- Design
- Implementation
- Testing
- User guide
- Evaluation
- Project report.

For this project, according to the AQA specification you are required to undertake:

a realistic problem for which there must be a real end user ...The problem will be of a substantial nature ... The emphasis will be on the project being an open system of a cyclic nature.

The difference between the AS project and the A2 project is this cyclical aspect; it is intended that your system should be reusable, day after day, month after month, year after year. It must therefore allow for deleting or archiving old data, and/or the setting up of forward data (e.g. a diary in a booking system).

The value of each of the project areas is as follows:

Analysis	18 marks	Design	16 marks
Implementation	15 marks	Testing	15 marks
User guide	8 marks	Evaluation	10 marks
Report	8 marks	**Total**	**90 marks**

1 Project considerations

There are a number of factors to consider when taking on a project and working within a project environment. Some of these considerations are shown in Figure 1.

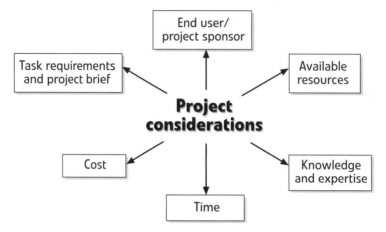

Figure 1

Project considerations

1.0 End user/project sponsor

This can be a single person, a department or an entire organisation. It is important that you have a single point of contact, as you will need to refer questions to this person on a regular basis, to ensure you are fulfilling requirements.

The end user/project sponsor will be the person or people who commission the project. They will provide a project brief identifying:

- the background to the problem
- project requirements
- scope of the project
- proposals for overcoming the problems identified
- information on users and resources upon which the project will impact
- project constraints, e.g. time or money.

You are accountable to the end user/project sponsor. You must ensure that you fulfil the requirements of the project brief and possibly report back at key stages on the progress made.

For your project, the end user cannot be yourself, your teacher or your best friend. It must be either

- a real end user, e.g. an employer, or someone else who needs a cyclical system, or
- an adult who can realistically role-play an end user.

1.1 Task requirements and project brief

The project brief will outline the requirements of the project and the expectations of the people commissioning it. These will be agreed with the developer (you), so that an agreed set of requirements can be developed and delivered.

If you are working on a project for a real end user, you may have time to deliver only part of what is needed; you must put the A2 module requirements first, and not spend all your time implementing, forgetting to produce the documentation and evaluation that make up nearly one third of the marks. Perhaps you can identify some functions that are not needed straight away.

1.2 Available resources

In order to meet the requirements of a given project, certain resources may be needed. These can include the following.

■ Hardware, on which to develop the project – this may be a combination of college and home machines. You must consider the facilities your user has to run the system when it is complete.

■ Software, with which to develop the system – this will most likely be a particular version of generic software. Again, consideration of version compatibility is important.

■ Money. How much does the user wish to spend? In a real-life situation, this is very important, as it constrains the amount of time that can be spent, as well as the software and hardware that can be used. For the A2 project, this may not be an issue.

■ Time. When does the user require the system to be implemented? In a real-life situation, this may be driven by outside forces such as legislation. Deadlines need to be decided and agreed right at the start of the project. Interim milestones should be set, too. For your project, there is an end date, set by the exam board. The amount of time you have available to spend on your project is a combination of available class time before the deadline and how much time you spend on it outside class.

■ People. As the developer, you need access to the person (or people) in control of the project, those who know the requirements, and also the end user(s) of the system – those who will use it on a daily basis. These may not be the same. In a veterinary surgery appointments system, for example, the project commissioner is likely to be the vet and/or practice manager, yet the reception staff and possibly even the veterinary nurses are likely to be end users as well.

1.3 Cost

This is a major consideration and a constraint for the majority of projects. How much will it cost to complete?

If you have been allocated a certain budget, you must ensure that all factors impacting upon the development and implementation of the project have been accounted for within that budget.

1.4 Knowledge and expertise

People who have a certain set of skills or expertise will undertake certain projects. For example, web designers and developers may not be allocated to a project that is developing an accounting system.

A project may consist of a number of different people who have been chosen to work within a project team, each contributing their own individual skills and expertise. Many companies have specialist testing teams, consisting of an analyst who draws up a test plan for each user requirement, plus a number of programmers who set up the test data and run the tests, correcting any errors and re-running the tests until the whole team is sure the system is error-free.

1.5 Time

This is a major issue, especially when a project has to be completed within a certain period. Time is also important when linked with cost, because time is money. The longer it takes to complete the project, the more delay is caused to operations and procedures, and this could cost an end user hundreds or even thousands of pounds.

All projects will follow a life-cycle that extends from the initial investigation through to the final evaluation and onto project maintenance, which could go on for years. A traditional project life-cycle model would include the following stages, which would provide these deliverables:

Stage	Deliverable(s)
User requirements	Requirements document, estimate, project plan
Analysis	System specification
Design	Design document
Program specification	Program/amendment specifications
Program build	Source code, test plan, results
System testing	Test plans/results
User acceptance testing	Support
Installation and implementation	Handover documents, support, review report

Mapping the A2 project requirements onto this traditional model gives the following stages and deliverables:

Stage	Deliverable(s)
Analysis	System specification. To contain statement of problem; context and nature of problem; user requirements specification; capabilities and limitations of resources; information flow and dynamics of current position; hardware and software capabilities and limitations; user training needs; evaluation criteria.
Design	Design document. To contain consideration of approaches, justifying final choice; detailed specification of input forms and screens; data validation required; processes and output screens and reports; project plan; test plan and test data.
Implementation	Annotated source code; initial test results.
Testing	Test results (evidence of corrections and re-runs).
User guide	User guide. To cover installation of the system; back-up procedures; general use; trouble-shooting; frequently asked questions.
Evaluation	Review report. To cover how system has addressed listed evaluation criteria, one by one; evidence of end-user involvement – could be user acceptance testing (data and results) or a signed affidavit.
Report	Technical handover documentation, suitable for someone else to follow steps taken during development, with annotated listings. Everything in a logical order, indexed.

When you are working on your own project solution it may help to set up a framework that you can follow to ensure that you have covered each step. By the end of the design stage you should have a project plan – keep it to hand and check progress against the plan regularly, at least once a week. Adjust the amount of time you are putting into the project if you are falling behind with your plan.

Many of the project stages for the A2 project, such as analysis, design and testing, are quite prescriptive in that you would need to ensure that they are completed in order to succeed with your solution.

Whereas in the AS project the implementation and testing stages were worth over half the project marks, this time they are worth just one third. This means that you have to put more effort into the other stages – analysis and design together are worth over a third, and the documentation and evaluation stages are worth just under a third.

You must put a lot of effort into the analysis tasks. It is important that you are clear what the problem is before you start doing detailed design and implementation. Therefore you will have to use formal methods for some of the analysis; it is no longer enough simply to list requirements and hope for the best.

2 Process skills – applications software

In order to meet the requirements of the project, you are expected to use applications software tools. *AS ICT for AQA* gives a review of the most-used generic packages on pages 184–195.

The specification says:

> To obtain high marks it is expected that the candidates' solution must accommodate the system's information flow and data dynamics. This might include data flows between packages, such as Dynamic Data Exchange.

Although it is perfectly acceptable for your system to be developed solely on one generic software package, it is also possible to design the system so that more than one will be used. For example:

- a web-based application that links to a relational database, making ticket bookings, updating seat/event availability, displaying availability to the web user
- a web-based ordering system which links to a relational database to create an order, update stock levels, automatically reorder, produce management sales reports, and so on
- a relational database application for stock control that has automatic reordering information exported into a spreadsheet format, for sending electronically to a supplier
- a relational database application for theatre-seat bookings that has a function sending data to a DTP package, to show seat availability graphically for the box office.

A database could send data to a DTP package for a box office

Here is a reminder of the capabilities of the most-used generic packages, and the features that are considered to be 'advanced'.

2.0 Word-processing

Obviously, you will be using a word-processing package (or DTP) to produce the documentation required. Make sure you use its facilities to best effect.

Activities where a word processor is useful include:

- producing standard templates
- producing logos and letterheads
- mail-merging documents
- producing documents that require specific formats, e.g. tables or columns
- basic desk-top publishing.

Advanced features of word-processing packages

Tables	Columns	Merging text and lists
Graphics	Watermarks	Templates
Indexing	Table of contents	Links/hyperlinks

2.1 Spreadsheet

For the A2 project, it is unlikely that solutions using only spreadsheets would allow for a fully reusable system; however, as part of the solution a spreadsheet could have many possibilities. Within organisations spreadsheets are used to:

- produce and display numerical, graphical and statistical data, such as:
  - sales forecasts
  - profit and loss accounts
  - general expenditure
  - wage and salary information
  - distribution facts
- forecast information
- calculate information
- analyse information
- automate procedures.

Advanced features of spreadsheet packages

Charts and graphs	Filtering/sorting	Pivot tables
Functions	Exporting/importing	OLE
Macros	Input forms/mechanisms	Ranges
Formulae	Multi-sheet workings	Auto start-up and close
Formatting	Locking and protection	

2.2 Database

Relational database software is the most commonly used software for A2 projects. This is because quite a sophisticated solution can be designed and implemented using it. It can cope with entity relationships, allowing information to be taken from a mix of data tables, and quite complex processing and reporting can take place.

Functions to initialise, enter, process, query and output data are available and straightforward to design and implement, and are in keeping with the A2 requirements for:

- some consideration of initialising the system
- clearing down data from previous use
- processing data
- transferring data such as logging transactions
- archiving data.

Advanced features of database packages

Import and export	Queries and reports from queries	Form Design Expert
Querying multiple tables	Forms designer	Report designer
Mailing labels	Custom reports	List boxes/combo boxes
Calculating values	Customising forms	Macros
Splash screens	Customising menus and icons	VBA programming (limited)
Importing data	Adding a graph	Mail merge
Switchboards	Relational database referential integrity	Primary and foreign key usage
Menu builder	Database administration	OLE
Dynamic Data Interchange	Application integration	Creating a runtime application

2.3 Multimedia

Multimedia software includes the use of sound, graphics and images or moving images. The most widely recognised multimedia platform is the Internet, as it incorporates each of these elements.

You could use the Internet to provide a web-based front end to your system – one that customers could use, rather than the end users within the business. It depends on what your system does as to how useful a web front end might be. There is no point producing a web-based system, or suggesting one to your project commissioner, if the system will not be used outside the business.

Remember that if you use borrowed HTML or JAVA code in the creation of your website, you must:

1 check for copyright permissions
2 acknowledge your source.

It is not within the current expectations of the ICT A Level for you to have to learn how to program for your project.

3 Analysis

In order to generate a solution that demonstrates a thorough understanding of both the users' needs and the applications software, consideration should be given to the following factors.

- Has the problem domain been fully investigated? Is it realistic?
- Has adequate time been allocated to each stage of the project?
- Has the current system been thoroughly and adequately investigated?
- Are adequate resources available to produce a detailed and complex solution specification?
- Have the precise needs of the users been identified?
- Have alternative solutions been considered?
- Is documentation adequate to take forward into the design stage, to enable final decisions to be made and a detailed design to be completed?

The analysis section carries a total of 18 marks. The criteria for gaining marks are shown below.

Maximum marks	Allocation of marks
15–18	■ The candidate has identified an appropriate problem in conjunction with the end user and independently of the teacher.
	■ A clear statement covering both the context and the nature of the problem has been provided.
	■ The candidate has clearly identified and delimited a substantial and realistic problem, recognising the requirements of the intended user(s) and the capabilities and limitations of the available resources.
	■ All of the requirements are specified and clearly documented.
	■ The candidate has fully identified the information flow and data dynamics of the problem.
	■ The analysis indicates understanding of the full potential of the appropriate hardware and software facilities which are available and, as appropriate, the limitations.
	■ The candidate has identified the user's current IT skill level and training needs.
	■ Qualitative and quantitative evaluation criteria have been identified in detail and analysis has been completed without undue assistance.
10–14	■ The candidate has identified an appropriate problem with reference to the end user and independently of the teacher.
	■ A clear outline statement covering both the context and the nature of the problem has been provided.
	■ The candidate has identified a substantial problem, recognising many of the requirements of the intended users and many of the capabilities and limitations of the available resources.
	■ The documentation is intelligible but is lacking in some respects.
	■ The analysis indicates which software will be used, but may not make it clear how the software will be used.

Maximum marks	Allocation of marks
	■ The candidate has partly identified the information flow and data dynamics of the problem.
	■ Reasonable evaluation criteria have been identified.
	■ Some assistance has been required to reach this stage.
	■ Alternatively, the candidate has identified a relatively straightforward problem and has proceeded unaided, covering most or all of the points required for 15–18 marks.
6–9	■ The candidate has required some guidance from the teacher to identify an appropriate problem with an end user.
	■ A simple outline statement has been provided.
	■ The candidate has selected a substantial problem and attempted to identify many of the requirements of the intended users and many of the capabilities and limitations of the resources available but has required assistance in analysing the problem.
	■ The candidate has identified only a limited subset of the information flow and data dynamics of the problem.
	■ The documentation is available but is incomplete.
	■ Alternatively, the candidate has identified a fairly simple problem and has recognised most of the requirements of the intended users and most of the capabilities and limitations of the resources available.
	■ The candidate has required assistance to analyse the problem.
	■ The documentation is complete in most respects.
3–5	■ The candidate required considerable guidance from the teacher to identify an appropriate problem with an end user.
	■ A superficial outline statement was provided.
	■ The candidate has identified a fairly simple problem, recognising some of the requirements of the intended users and some of the capabilities and limitations of the available resources.
	■ Few, if any, indications of what must be done to carry out the task are present.
	■ There is little indication of how the software will be used.
	■ The candidate has not identified the information flow and data dynamics of the problem.
	■ Documentation is weak and incomplete.
	■ The candidate has required much assistance in analysing the problem.
1–2	■ The candidate has identified a simple problem or been given a straightforward problem.
	■ There is only minimal recognition of either the requirements of the intended users or capabilities and limitations of the available resources.
	■ The documentation is poor and substantial assistance has been required.
0	■ No analysis is present.

Interpretation of analysis requirements

Analysis (18)	15–18	10–14	6–9	3–5	1–2
Problem identification	Clear statement covering context and nature	Clear outline statement covering context and nature	Simple outline statement	Considerable guidance from teacher	Simple problem
Requirements analysis	All clearly identified independently	Most clearly identified independently	Assistance needed to specify full requirements	Some requirements identified	Minimal requirements identified
Data analysis	Data dynamics fully identified	Data dynamics partly identified	Limited data analysis or information flow	Some data analysis or information flow	Little mention
Resource analysis	Full potential of resources recognised	Most capabilities of resources recognised	Most capabilities of resources recognised	Statement of hardware and software, some discussion	Statement of hardware and software, no discussion
User skill level/ training needs	Current levels identified	General statements on skill levels	Little mention	Little mention	Little mention
Evaluation criteria	Detailed qualitative and quantitative criteria identified	Reasonable criteria identified	Some criteria, reasonable detail	Some criteria, little detail	At least one criterion

3.0 Problem identification

To produce a clear problem statement, at least one meeting with the end user must have taken place. There may be a document, a list of requirements or you may have to discuss their requirements, taking notes. This part of the analysis does not need to be long – most problems can be set out in under a page of A4.

The format of the problem identification should be:

- background of the company, what they do, the main personnel within the company
- background to the problem, whether there is an existing system, manual or computerised, why this does not now meet the business's needs
- a short statement as to what is required of a new system
- the people involved in the development process and in the new system – managers, users, etc; how they will use it, when and in what capacity.

An example is shown below.

Problem statement

Hightown Auto repairs has been in business for 15 years. It is run by brothers Barry and Jack Wilding. They do all types of car repair, but are known locally as experts in bodywork and have a reputation for performing excellent repair work on top-class cars.

Their interest in high-quality cars has led them to invest in a stretch limousine, which they hire out to people for special occasions such as weddings. It is something of a hobby, and one or other of the brothers drives the limo in turn.

They have four other people working for them, all of whom take bookings for both car repairs and limousine rides. There is a desktop PC, five years old, on which they have customer and job records systems, an accounting package and a simple stock-control package for parts.

Recently demand has started to rise and they have been turning down business, so they are considering buying another limo this month and a further two in six months time. While there was only one car, any bookings were simply put into the bookings diary with the other bodywork jobs, always at the top of the page so it was obvious each day what was required.

Barry, the business manager, has realised that before they can operate what will be a fleet of limousines for hire, they need to organise a proper booking system. They will have to recruit some new drivers and will need to be able to keep them busy with bookings. If it takes off as he hopes it will, they may need to recruit a receptionist/administrative assistant.

Barry will be the main contact during development, although Jack, as repair shop manager, will also wish to be involved. For the time being they are likely to be the main users of the system – certainly they will want to see trends of usage and so on to decide when to expand, judge how much profit they are making on the cars, and so on. The booking function will have to be easy enough for any of the current workers to use, as whoever answers the phone may have to use it, and currently only Barry uses the PC.

3.1 Requirements analysis

The user's requirements are the most important element of the analysis; therefore finding out exactly what is wanted from the system is the first step in producing a solution to the problem.

Using interviewing and other investigation techniques which you will have employed for your AS project (summarised on pages 148–9), you should be able to produce all the elements for a successful analysis, including a list of requirements.

Requirements are likely to be of various types. Some will be physical/measurable, such as 'provide a list of all cars repaired this week', or quantifiable. Some requirements will be less concrete, such as 'it must have easy-to-use input screens' or 'a logical order of processes', both of which are subjective, or qualitative, to a certain degree.

Some typical requirements for a video hire shop would be:

Requirements

Quantitative

The system should be able to:

- list borrowers
- list borrowers in a specified order (alphabetic, by post code, etc.)
- mail-merge letters, or print address labels
- edit borrower details (add, delete, change details)
- record loans of items
- update accounts after each loan
- update stock availability after each loan
- record return of items
- add a new video to stock
- update stock after a delivery
- show which items are out on loan
- show which items are overdue
- show who owes money.

Qualitative

The system should:

- be quick to load up
- be easy to use
- be secure, password protected
- require minimum IT skills and training
- have clear fonts
- use colours in a helpful way – not dazzling
- use sounds to get attention, but not intrusively
- use navigation buttons with a consistent layout and colour scheme
- have a clear and easy-to-understand manual
- have diagrams in the manual
- use plain English in the manual, with any jargon clearly explained
- show solutions to common problems in the manual
- have automatic back-ups – or clearly explain how to do them.

3.2 Investigation techniques

Whatever the source of the problem, a thorough investigation should take place to ensure that all the necessary information has been gathered for the project design.

There are a number of established investigative techniques that aid data collection. These are sometimes referred to as **fact-finding techniques**. They include the ones shown in Figure 2.

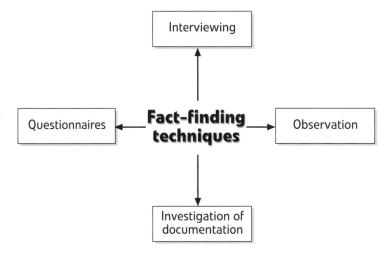

Figure 2

Fact-finding techniques

Interviewing

Interviewing end users is in some cases the best way to gather information about the requirements for the new system. Ask questions such as:

- Can you clearly outline the problem?
- How many and what type of user does the problem impact upon?
- Does the problem impact upon other systems or tasks?
- What solutions do you have to overcome the problem?
- Are there any constraints that could impact upon any proposals given?

Answers to these will provide you with a detailed overview of the environment and issues relating to the system. Interviewing may also give you the opportunity to prioritise what needs to be done, and when.

By interviewing users, you can ensure that the information already received is correct, gather new information, and have the opportunity to understand the system better through the eyes of the user.

Questionnaires

Questionnaires are sometimes a more convenient way of collecting information, normally because it would be too time-consuming for all potential users to be interviewed.

The benefits of using a questionnaire include:

- it provides a documentary record of wants and needs
- it is flexible and convenient
- it can be given to a number of users simultaneously
- it is a mass data collection tool.

Questionnaires are an excellent way of gathering and also consolidating information, provided that the following conditions are met:

- ✓ the questionnaire is structured appropriately
- ✓ a control mechanism is in place for gathering up the questionnaires
- ✓ the correct user group has been targeted.

The questionnaire should be set out clearly to provide opportunities for both short answers based on facts and figures, and descriptive answers. A balance of questions will ensure that you collect all of the information required to continue with your investigation.

It is always best to provide a time limit for the return of questionnaires, such as 'Please return within three working days'. Another way to ensure that the questionnaire is returned is to ask users to fill them in and then collect them yourself.

When designing a questionnaire a vital factor to consider is who the questionnaire is aimed at. The target audience is very important because users can interpret a question very differently depending on their status and the role they play within the system.

Observation

For some task-related problems that are quite dynamic, it may be more convenient to observe the end user and all the processes that lead from data collection through data entry, data processing, output production and output dissemination. Manual processes are often best investigated by using observation. This will enable you to see first-hand what is going on, the issues and the type of environment and conditions under which a new system would need to operate.

Investigation of documentation

Depending on your end user/project sponsor, you may find that you are given a range of documentation to help you plan your project. This may be especially true if you have a real, organisational-based end user.

If for example you were carrying out an investigation on a specific functional department within an organisation, such as finance, suggesting ways of increasing efficiency in the payroll system, documentation that you could be given includes:

- an organisational chart
- a breakdown of personnel within the department
- job roles and descriptions of finance personnel
- sample forms used in the payroll system
- lists of procedures that are carried out on a daily basis by finance personnel.

Investigation of the documentation in this case would give you an overall picture of what is done, how it is done and by whom. You may indeed have to use other fact-finding methods to collect more detailed information, but at least you would have a starting point to direct your investigation.

3.3 Analysis of the problem domain

Once the fact-finding investigation has been carried out, the next stage in the project development would be to analyse the information that has been collected. Depending on how much information you have, you could present the analysis in a written format – outlining your findings step by step and documenting stages of your investigation. An alternative method would be to present the analysis in a visual format – illustrating the relationship between end users, task dependencies and the overall systems environment.

A context diagram (or level 0 data-flow diagram, as it is also known) can give a graphical view of the existing system with all its interfaces. A sample context diagram for a simple appointment-booking system is shown in Figure 3.

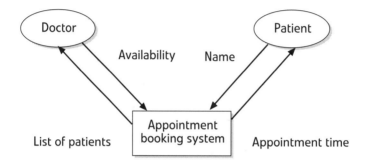

Figure 3

Context diagram

The context diagram clearly shows the interfaces between the system under investigation and the external entities with which it communicates. Therefore, while it is often simple, a context diagram serves to focus attention on the system boundary and can help in clarifying the precise scope of the analysis.

Flow diagrams can be used to illustrate the steps or processes and how they interact. For example, using the set of processes in Figure 4, below, where would you add arrows to see which processes follow which, which interact with which, and so on?

1 Patient telephones or calls into reception for appointment	**2** Doctor sends a list of available surgery times to be added to the diary
3 A suitable time is found in the diary and the patient's name is recorded	**4** A list of all patients to be seen in each surgery is given to the doctor, together with patient notes

Figure 4

Set of processes

Clearly process 3 follows process 1, and process 4 follows process 3. Where does process 2 fit into the flow? It is really the first process, as appointments cannot be made without an empty diary. But it is also a process that has to be done on a regular basis.

These diagrams need to be drawn using trial and error, so don't do them straight onto the computer – paper and pencil is the best way, until you are sure you have it right. There are some drawing packages available that make drawing up data-flow and other diagrams simpler than trying to use the drawing facilities of a generic package.

The use of diagrams to illustrate any problems in the existing system can have a number of advantages over a written analysis. These include:

- there is no need to write large amounts of notes
- it gives a clearer overview of what is happening with the entire system
- it is easy to identify key elements within the system such as:
  - information types
  - information flows
  - storage mechanisms
  - users
- it is easier to identify relationships and working patterns within the system.

Apart from the information flows, the data dynamics of the existing system need to be documented. The areas that need explaining, whether in written or visual format, are:

- inputs and their sources
- processes
- data stores
- data flows between processes, stores, sources and output destinations
- outputs and their destinations
- the scope, or what is included and what is excluded from this system.

What may also become clear while you are doing this is that other systems provide data for this one, or need to receive data from this one. For example, a stock-control system may provide data for the accounting system or the purchasing system.

Once you have broken down the current system, it should be easy to identify the problems with using it. Most end users will have given you lists of problems that have to be analysed in the light of all your findings. When you are devising possible solutions, you must remember to take all concerns into account, while aiming to focus on the main requirements.

3.4 Data analysis

Identifying the data needed for the business to operate is the next step. You need to find out where the data comes from, what information is produced as a result of processing that data, and who the output goes to.

Data-flow diagrams are the best way of showing how data works in a system.

The notation used in one structured analysis technique is shown in Figure 5.

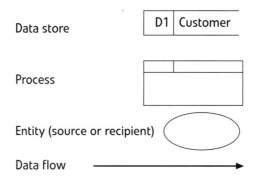

Data store	D1	Customer
Process	
Entity (source or recipient)	
Data flow	

Figure 5

Data-flow notation

What does this mean?

Data store: Any place where data is held. In a manual system this may be in an address book, a directory, or a set of invoices; in a computer it is generally a file of some sort.

Process: Any action that causes something to happen to some data, making a change or converting it into information. In a manual system this could be looking up a phone number in a directory, writing a phone number down in an address book, or calculating a total and putting it at the bottom of an invoice. In a computer it could be automatic calculation of the total, or producing a list of patients and appointment times. All processes have input and output – something going in and something coming out. With data-flow diagrams, it is processes involving data that are included.

Data flow: Used to show how data moves into, between and out of processes, and between sources and recipients (destination) of data. These may be people, institutions or other systems. Data flow is not the physical article but the data that accompanies it – not the stock item itself, but the order, the picking list, the delivery note, the bill and/or the receipt.

Sources of data: Those *external entities* that provide data for the system. These may be customers, who provide order details, or suppliers, who provide delivery notes and invoices.

Recipients (destinations) of data: Those *external entities* who receive output from the system, but do not directly use it. For example, government departments receive tax returns from payroll systems, and VAT returns from accounting systems; the board of governors at a school receives performance and financial reports.

Data-flow diagrams can be drawn at different levels, to show levels of process. If a process is not a single step, a further diagram is required to show the breakdown. Each process is numbered, with the system being numbered 0.

An example for a catalogue system is shown in Figures 6, 7 and 8 on the next pages. Figure 6 shows basic data flow from customer to system.

Figure 6

Context diagram

© Tony Drewry, University of the West of England

The level 1 data-flow diagram (DFD) in Figure 7 breaks the system into three main processes, the first to check whether the customer is credit-worthy, the second to deal with the order of goods, finding them, picking them and sending them to the customer, and the third to maintain the credit details held for existing customers. The arrow with the question mark indicates that there needs to be some input for this process, but as yet, the analyst does not know who or where this will come from.

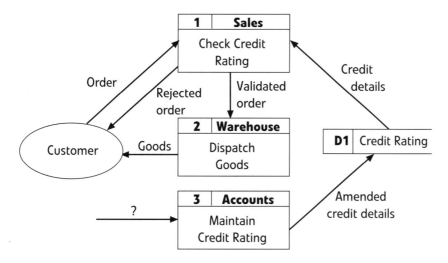

Figure 7

Level 1 data-flow diagram

© Tony Drewry, University of the West of England

The level 2 DFD for process 1 is shown in Figure 8 on the next page. Process 2 is likely to break down to at least one more level as well, more likely two or three more levels. Notice how the numbering system works. The lines surrounding this DFD show the boundaries of the process – the external entity 'Customer' and the data store 'Credit rating' are held outside the process.

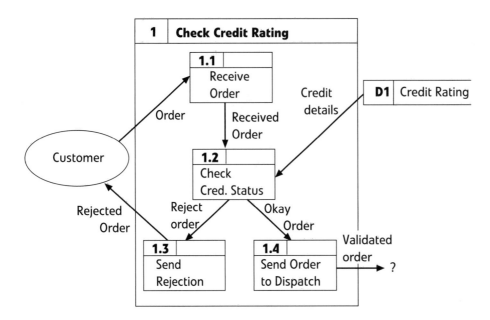

Figure 8

Level 2 data-flow diagram

© Tony Drewry, University of the West of England

Data-flow diagrams may be used for documenting the current system, but are more useful when designing the proposed system.

3.5 Resource analysis

From your interviews and observations, it is important to identify the resources available and those that may be needed in the future.

The statement of resource availability must include hardware and software currently available but also the potential for upgrading, adding to the system, using the network, and so on. Not every business will require either nothing adding to their existing system, or a completely new one, so your analysis should evaluate what is needed in this situation.

Other resources to consider are the people involved, their talents and experience. Only by careful investigation are you likely to discover what knowledge is already held. Sometimes people don't realise that they hold the key to unlocking a long-term problem with the procedures in their company.

Sometimes there is one person who has had full responsibility for the current system for many years and is the only person who knows it inside out. A replacement system cannot be developed without input from this person, who may have moved on. The availability of that person then becomes an issue.

3.6 User skill level/training needs

A list of people who will be involved with the new system is needed, with a short pen-picture of their role in the new system, their general skill levels with computer systems, and any basic training needs as well as any specific training needs for the new system. An example is shown below.

Training needs

Seema is the evening receptionist. Currently her work is all manual, but she has been on a college course to learn basic IT skills and has a CLAIT qualification, so she has some confidence with a keyboard and mouse. She will be one of the main users for the appointments system, so will need training straight away in how to set up the empty diary, how to make appointments and how to get reports from the system for the doctors.

3.7 Evaluation criteria

This is a list that can be used once the system has been implemented, to see whether it matches the users' specifications. It is normally based on the list of user requirements, possibly with some performance criteria included, such as 'response time of < 1 second is required'.

The list must be clearly divided into quantitative and qualitative criteria – those criteria that are measurable (even Yes or No is acceptable), and those which are less easy to evaluate as they are subjective measures. The best way to evaluate a criterion such as 'easy to use' may be by asking a selection of users to try out the system then fill in a questionnaire.

3.8 Sign-off

Once the analysis is complete, with user requirements and evaluation criteria, then your client/user should be given the document to read and approve.

A meeting should be arranged where you, as the analyst, can talk through the proposed system to gain agreement before any detailed design work takes place. It is easier to make changes at this stage than to leave it until later. Once the user is happy with the proposed system, the design stage can start.

For evidence, have a sign-off sheet drawn up and ask your user to sign it – an example is given is Figure 9 opposite. Keep notes of any meetings and any evidence that you have made changes to your system. The more evidence you have of involvement by your user, the better.

Bedrooms 4 You Order System

Date	Meeting to discuss	Attendees	Comments/Actions	Approval (Doc sign-off only)
10/10/2003	Analysis	A User, S Analyst	1. Add link to accounts 2. Add 2 reports	
17/10/2003	Analysis	A User, S Analyst	Analysis approved	A User
15/11/2003	Design	A User, S Analyst	1. No test plan yet 2. Put date on each screen 3. Order number formatted on reports	
22/11/2003	Design	A User, S Analyst	1. No test plan 2. Detailed design approved 3. Work schedule approved	A User, A User

Figure 9

Sample sign-off sheet

4 Design

The design phase brings together all of the results of the analysis to generate a range of possible solutions. These alternative solutions may be using different packages or a different range of packages, or merely different solutions within one package.

The aim of design is to provide a specification with enough detail so that any competent person could take it away and implement the system you have designed, coming up with exactly the same system. There needs to be a clear specification of how each sub-task identified in the analysis stage is to be completed.

The design stage is worth 16 marks. The criteria for gaining the marks are shown below.

Maximum marks	Allocation of marks
13–16	■ A relevant range of appropriate approaches to a solution has been considered in detail. Compelling reasons for final choice of solution are given which have been fully justified and the likely effectiveness has been fully considered. ■ A completely detailed solution has been specified so that it could be undertaken by a competent third party. The proposed solution has been clearly broken down into sub-tasks, with the necessary indications of how those are to be solved. All the requirements are specified and clearly documented. ■ A well-defined schedule and work plan have been included, showing in detail how the task is to be undertaken. This explains what is required in a comprehensible manner – it can include layout sheets, record structures, spreadsheet plans, design for data-capture sheets, as appropriate. ■ An effective and full testing plan has been devised, with a comprehensive selection of test data and reasons for the choice of the data clearly specified. ■ This stage has been undertaken without assistance.
9–12	■ A relevant range of appropriate approaches to a solution has been considered. Reasons for final choice of solution are provided which have been justified and the likely effectiveness has been reasonably considered. ■ A solution has been specified which a competent third party could carry out, but with some difficulty. The proposed solution is broken down into sub-tasks, with some indication of how those are to be solved. Some of the requirements are specified and clearly documented. ■ A schedule and work plan has been included, showing how the tasks are to be undertaken. This explains what is required in a reasonable manner – it can include layout sheets, record structures, spreadsheet plans, design for data-capture sheets, as appropriate. ■ A testing plan has been devised, with some tests clearly specified. ■ This stage has been undertaken without undue assistance.
6–8	■ A limited range of approaches which may have required some assistance. The reasons given for the final choice are weak and the likely effectiveness has not been discussed in detail.

Maximum marks	Allocation of marks
	■ Sufficient detail has been given so that the candidate, but not another person, can replicate the solution at a later date. An attempt has been made to break down the solution into sub-tasks, with some indications of how these are to be solved. The documentation is clear but lacking in some respects.
	■ A schedule and work plan are included but limited in nature.
	■ A testing plan is present.
	■ This has been undertaken without undue assistance.
3–5	■ Only one approach considered which may have required considerable assistance. Only vague reasons given for the final choice and the likely effectiveness has not been discussed.
	■ Sufficient detail has been given so that the candidate, but not another person, can replicate the solution at a later date, but with some difficulty. An attempt has been made to break down the solution into sub-tasks but with insufficient indications as to how those are to be solved. The documentation is lacking in many respects.
	■ A schedule and work plan should be included, but are poorly thought out.
	■ A testing plan is included but is poor.
	■ Substantial assistance may have been required.
1–2	■ Little or no consideration has been given to approaches to the solution. No or invalid reasons given for final choice of solution.
	■ A superficial outline of the solution has been chosen so that the candidate is unable to replicate the solution at a later date. Little attempt has been made to break down the problem into sub-tasks.
	■ The schedule and work plan are vague or missing. The testing plan is vague or missing. The documentation is poor and substantial assistance may have been required.
0	■ No detail of chosen solution given.

Interpretation of design requirements

Design (16)	13–16	9–12	6–8	3–5	1–2
Solution consideration	Relevant range of approaches considered in detail	Relevant range of approaches considered	Limited range of approaches	Only one approach	Little or no consideration given
Solution design	Third party could carry it out exactly as specified	Third party could carry it out with difficulty	Sufficient detail for candidate to replicate later	Sufficient detail for candidate to replicate later, with difficulty	Superficial outline, no replication possible, even for candidate
Schedule/ work plan	Well defined in detail	Included, showing tasks	Present, but limited	Present, poorly thought out	Vague or missing
Input design	All inputs and data capture forms in accurate detail	All inputs and data capture forms evident	Most inputs and data capture forms evident	Some inputs and data capture forms evident	Vague or missing
Output design	All outputs in accurate detail	All outputs evident	Most outputs evident	Some outputs evident	Vague or missing
Processing design	All processes explained in detail	All processes evident	Most processes evident	Some processes evident	Vague or missing
Test planning	Comprehensive, covering all functions with extreme, normal and erroneous data	All functions covered with extreme, normal and erroneous data	All functions covered	Some functions covered	Vague or missing
Test data/ expected results	Complete and matching plan	Mostly complete, cross-referenced to plan	Mostly complete	Some data and expected results	Vague or missing

4.0 Solution consideration

The design section should be introduced by a discussion about the different technical and practical options and which has been chosen, with reasons both for rejection and for acceptance. This discussion follows on from the resource implications section in the analysis, so make sure you tie them up.

For example, the hardware, software and budget that your user has may not allow for additional packages to be bought, so a proposed purchase may not be allowed; there may not be reliable Internet accessibility, so a website may not be practical; or the requirements mean that a particular option is unwise and may not deliver what the user wants.

This is your final decision – everything you design after this is geared towards using the software and hardware that you have specified here.

Somewhere in this section there needs to be a table indicating the exact technical specification to be used (hardware, software and communications facilities). For a single-user system, this may be the existing system owned by the client; for a networked system, this may need to hold further technical details.

The specification of the development system should also be explained – if the development environment is significantly different from the operational environment, the test plan must allow for testing the system in the operational situation before it can be signed off.

4.1 Solution design

This category spans all the design detail, not only the input, output and processing design as detailed separately below. This must include all the information that is needed to implement your solution in the way you have designed it.

Top marks are available only if the design could be taken away by anyone at this point, and implemented without having to come back to you for advice and guidance.

What is needed therefore is a complete breakdown of all items to be included, and also instructions on how they are to be implemented.

The items should include:

- data capture methods
- data capture forms
- input screen layouts
- a menu and screen/function hierarchy
- data breakdown (entity-relationship diagram)
- data dictionary (keys identified)
- data storage method
- processing and calculations, spelt out using structured English, flowcharts or other methods
- output screen layouts
- output printed report layouts
- output methods and dissemination
- test plans, data and expected results.

The methods should include:

- a list of all functions, and the screen, data and/or output they use
- a standard way of naming data items
- a standard way of writing any code required
- a standard way for positioning fields on screens, or reports (e.g. having current data showing top right)
- the order of implementation.

One way to show high-level analysis and design skills is to have a contents page for each section of your project and to keep items in a logical order.

4.2 Schedule/work plan

Having a project plan is a requirement of this project. It does not have to be produced in a project-planning package if one is not available, but plans produced in such a way do tend to look more professional.

If you have taken the time to create the detailed list of items to be produced on implementation, then making the task list for the plan is simple. Extras that you must include are to schedule meetings with your user on a regular basis, and to allow time at various stages for printing and checking, especially near the end. It is also advisable to include a period for error correction and re-running of tests.

With your list of tasks, and assuming that you are the only resource for the implementation, you need to estimate the time needed to undertake each task. Work in hours and be realistic. For example, designing a screen with around 12 data items on it will take around 2 hours, by the time you are happy with it; printing out an entire report might take 1 hour plus numbering time, plus time to set up the contents page properly – probably a good 2–3 hours, right at the end.

Once you have listed all your tasks, with the amount of time needed, you know how much work is involved. This is the time to schedule. Start with the dates you must meet – the final hand-in date, user meeting dates, any other milestones you have been given. Now see how much time you need between these dates and apportion your time accordingly.

Identify tasks you must do on a computer and those that can be done by hand (for example, screen and report designs do not need to be machine produced).

Identify tasks you must do on college machines (perhaps because of the software being used) and those you could do at home (for example, you could produce the test plan or start the user guide at home).

When you have sorted out the order in which the tasks can be done, the schedule needs to be drawn up properly. There are two ways of doing this. You can use a simple table, showing task, time, order, dates, etc., or for a better visual effect, draw up (or use project software to produce) a Gantt chart.

Identify tasks you must do on computers at college

	Stage/Task	No of Hours effort	Week begining 1-12	8-12	15-12	22-12	29-12	5-01	12-01	19-01	26-01	2-02	9-02	16-02	23-02
5	**Implementation & Testing**														
6	Create Database structures	4													
7	Input form 1 - build & test	4													
8	Input form 2 - build & test	4													
9	Input form 3 - build & test	4													
10	Report 1 - Build & test	2													
11	Report 2 - Build & test	2													
12	Report 3 - Build & test	3													
13	Query 1 - build & test	3													
14	Query 2 - build & test	2													
15	Query 3 - build & test	4													
16	Menu system	2													
17	System test	12													
18	User test	5													
19	Rework/retest	8													
20	User signoff	1													
21															
22	**User Guide**														
23	Installation Procedures	2													
24	Intro	2													
25	Navigation	2													
26	Instructions for each function	15													
27	End of day/month/year	3													
28	Backup procedures	3													
29	Pull together Guide	2													
30															
31	**Evaluation**														
32															
33	**Report**														
34	Finish off	4													
35	Bind	1													

Figure 10

A sample Gantt chart

4.3 Input design

This is not only about screen design, although that is a major part of what you need to do. Data capture forms, if being redesigned as part of your system, are also required. This section should also include where the data is coming from – for example, a delivery list of videos may provide the data for input on the designed screen in Figure 11 below. It may be that not all of the data required is present on this delivery note, so that other data has to be gathered from elsewhere. This needs to be spelt out field by field, so that the data entry clerk knows what to put in each field on the screen.

For data capture forms, it is not only the look that is important but also the design of the paper – will it be A4 or A5 in size, will it be on a pad or loose, will there be numbers pre-printed (e.g. for invoices), what colour and thickness of paper should be used, does the company need more than one copy (therefore two- or three-part paper)? Design issues include using the company logo, name and address, any pre-printed warnings or instructions, as well as adequate space for all the fields that are required. If it is an order form, it may translate onto more than one data input screen (one for the header detail, one for each item). It is important that the two match as far as possible.

Figure 11

A sample data entry form

Screen design

The first thing that must be done is to decide on a look for the screens – this is the user interface, so consistency and professionalism are required.

- Design a standard layout, showing company name and logo, system name and function (screen) title, date, and screen reference, using the same colours and fonts to indicate the same type of field or element.
- If you are using buttons, decide on the shape, size and colour to be used. For any function buttons, e.g. navigation or calculation functions that will be part of the screen, make sure there is a standard place and icon/button in use for each one.

If you are hand drawing the screens, make sure they are to scale. As for all designs, another person should be able to take your designs and produce exactly the same screen that you would have done.

For each input field, there should be the following information:

- size
- where it comes from (entity/table name, field name, calculated)
- any validation that should be performed.

A sample screen design (produced in a spreadsheet package for a project that is to be implemented in a database package) is shown in Figure 12.

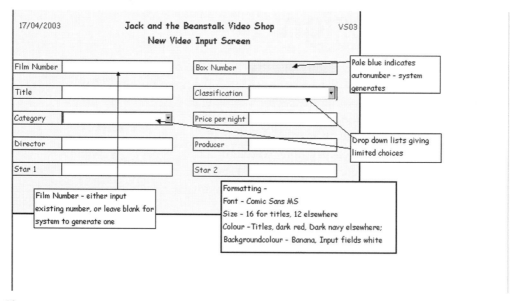

Figure 12

Sample screen design

Another diagram that should be included as part of the input design is a menu and screen hierarchy, showing how each of the functions is found.

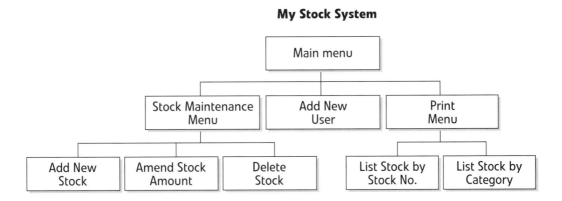

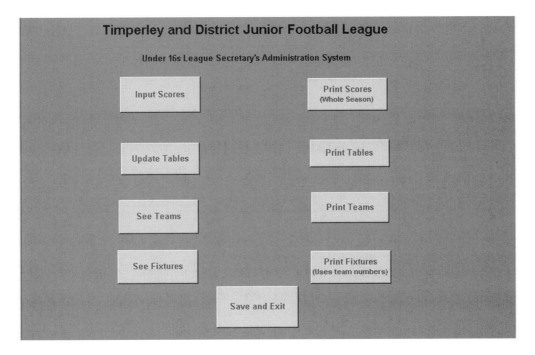

Figure 13

A sample menu and function hierarchy

The main menu and any sub-menus also need a screen design to be included.

Figure 14

A sample menu design

4.4 Output design

As with the requirements of input design, this is not merely about layouts for screens and printed reports. Consideration also needs to be given to the data/information fields on each, where they come from, how they are to be displayed and so on. A very important field to have on a printed report is the date it was printed, in case it goes astray, or a re-run happens after some data changes.

For each output printed report, you need to be clear who is the recipient, whether more than one copy is required, and so on. Some situations may mean that different types of output are considered – for example, output onto a hand-held PDA, or printing onto special paper or card if the report is likely to be used outdoors. There should be an indication of how big the paper is (a receipt would not necessarily be designed for A4 paper), the number of lines that can be shown per page for long reports, and so on. If known, the printer to be used can be allowed for – if you know there is a colour printer, you may wish to design colour into the report to differentiate or highlight data.

Again, as for the input design, everything must be spelt out so that someone else could take these designs and produce the functions that create the output screen or report.

Remember that enquiry functions are a combination of input and output – normally one or two fields are input and a lot of information is output to screen, sometimes with an option to print. Include them in only one place.

As with the screen designs, report designs should show the standard look for the system and the company.

Figure 15 shows a list report that is likely to be more than one page long. The main processing steps are also included in this design.

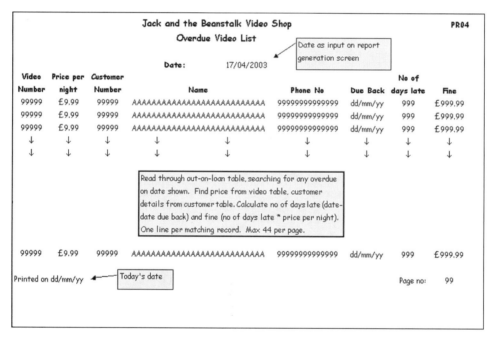

Figure 15

A sample printed report design

4.5 Processing design

This section consists of all processing and calculations, plus exactly what data is being input, calculated, processed and output at every stage of your system.

Data breakdown

At the analysis stage, data-flow diagrams were drawn up, so data sources, sinks and stores have already been identified. At the design stage it is necessary to refine these data stores, or entities, and to construct the best database possible for this data.

See pages 94–5 for entity relationships. *AS ICT for AQA* goes into detail about entities and relationships, and entity-relationship diagrams for a database system, on pages 205–209. As most projects will be based on a database model, whatever software is being used, an entity-relationship diagram and a data dictionary will be required.

What does this mean?	
Entity:	Something that data is stored about, for example a customer, supplier, employee, patient, video and so on. The data stored about the entity are the **attributes** of that entity. For a video, these might be title, director, rating, stars, genre.
Relationship:	That which links entities together. There are three types: one-to-one, one-to-many and many-to-many.

At the design stage, only two types of relationship are allowed – one-to-one and one-to-many, so any rationalisation of many-to-many relationships will have to take place. An example is shown in Figure 16.

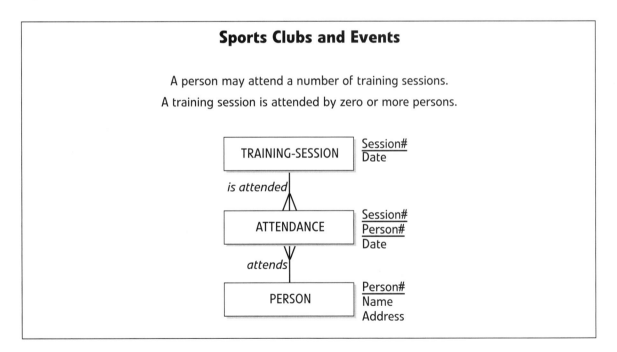

Figure 16

Entity relationships

© Tony Drewry, University of the West of England

The main attributes are identified along with any keys that appear in that entity.

These attributes are put into a table or list known as the data dictionary. Each attribute, or field, appears only once, as part of the information associated with it is a column that shows where and how it is used in the database.

Examples of an entity-relationship diagram, entity list and attribute list for a library management system are shown in Figures 17, 18 and 19.

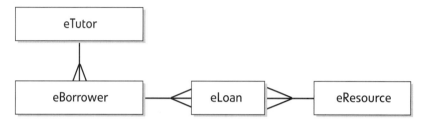

Figure 17

Entity-relationship diagram for library management system

Name	Description	Attributes	Relationships
eTutor	Table that holds name and location details about tutors	**TutorID** Name Staffroom ExtNo	One-to-many with eBorrower
eBorrower	Table that holds name and contact details about Borrowers	**BorrowerID** Name Address PhoneNo TutorID	One-to-many with eLoan
eLoan	Table that has details of who borrowed what	**LoanID** BorrowerID ResourceID DateDueBack	
eResource	Table that holds details of each resource	**ResourceID** Type Title Author Price LoanPeriod	One-to-many with eLoan

Figure 18

Entity list

Name	Description	Type (length)	Validation	Where used
Address	Borrower's address	Text(75)	Must be present	Attribute in eBorrower
Author	Resource Author/ producer	Text(30)	Must be present	Attribute in eResource
BorrowerID	Borrower's unique identity	Number(9)	Must be present	Primary key of eBorrower, also as foreign key in eLoan
DateDueBack	Date resource is due to be returned	Date(10)	Format DD/ MM/YYYY	Attribute in eLoan
ExtNo	Phone extension for tutor	Number(4)	Must be present	Attribute in eTutor
LoanPeriod	No of days item usually on loan	Number(2)	Range 4–28	Attribute in eResource
Name	Name of person	Text(30)	Must be present	Attribute used in eBorrower, eTutor
PhoneNo	Phone number	Text(13)		Attribute used in eBorrower
ResourceID	Unique identifier for resource	Number(11)	Must be present	Primary key of eResource, foreign key in eLoan
StaffRoom	Staff room identity	Text(6)	Must be present	Attribute in eTutor
Title	Resource title	Text(30)	Must be present	Attribute in eResource
TutorID	Unique identifier for tutor	Number(9)	Must be present	Primary key of eTutor, foreign key in eBorrower
Type	Type of resource	Text(1)	B,C,V	Attribute in eResource

Figure 19
Attribute list

Processing and calculations

Every process must have its processing written down in some way – you could use diagrams or flowcharts, step-by-step English instructions or more formal pseudocode. It depends on the project and the software. For each process you also need to indicate which input screen, which output screen or report and what data it is using, so all these things need including.

With generic software, most packages allow the recording of macros. The steps for each macro need to be written down, so that another developer could create the macro that you envisaged during design, and attach it to the button you designed. The name of each macro must also be decided on, for the same reason.

For example, when designing a query in a database package, there will be a screen design, and one or more tables, but perhaps only some of the attributes in them; some fields may be calculated, and there may be a sub-form. This could all be one process to provide particular information based on some criteria. See Figure 20 on next page.

```
Process:      LRCP12 – Query overdue books
Input:        Pop-up screen LRCSI21
Output:       Screen out LRCSO09
Data:         eLoan (read-only)
              eBorrower (read-only)
              eResource (read-only)
              eTutor (read-only)
Steps:        Open all files
              Display pop-up screen
              Accept ReportingDate
              Write header details to Output screen
              Set Linecount to 0
              For each entry on eLoan Do
                      If DateDueBack < ReportingDate then
                      If ResourceType = "B" then
                              Get BorrowerName from eBorrower
                              Get Resource Title from eResource
                              Get TutorDetails from eTutor
                              Add 1 to Linecount
                              If Linecount < 21 then
                                      Write a detail line to output screen
                              Else
                                      Write continue message to output screen
                                      If continue then
                                              Set linecount to 1
                                              Clear detail area on screen
                                              Write a detail line to output screen
                                      Endif
                              Endif
                      Endif
                      Endif
              End Loop (get next eLoan entry)
```

Figure 20

Database query

4.6 Test planning

What is test planning?

Test planning involves creating documents that, according to the relevant ANSI/IEEE standard, 'describe the scope, approach, resources and schedule of intended testing activities. Test plans identify test items, the features to be tested, the testing tasks, who will do each task and any risks requiring contingency planning.'

Test plans are useful tools to organise, manage and schedule the testing effort. A well-thought-out test plan can greatly facilitate the testing work. Just as you need plans from an architect to build a house and guide the efforts of the builders, plumbers and electricians, you need a test plan to accomplish the same for your testing effort.

Test planning should allow for all levels of testing – at unit level each button is tested as you create it, each query is tested to a certain extent, each function, the whole system, and at some point, before you have finished, your users should also test it using their own data (although you may have to provide this under their supervision).

You need to make sure that data written to a file or table in one function can be read by the next or subsequent functions. The purpose of testing is to 'provoke failure'. You are not proving it works, you are out to prove it does not – to find the errors. Hence tests have to be planned to check out every path through the system, every option button, every combination of If statements, every field that has validation on it, and so on.

The following example is a strategy (high-level plan) for a website, rather than a database system, but this shows how much testing effort will be required even for a system that has no data.

WW-hire website – Test plan

▓ Check html syntax for all html files	– test 1
▓ Check all files free of viruses	– test 2

Do following checks in Internet Explorer AND Netscape Navigator

▓ Check site loads initially	– test 3
▓ Check all links and navigation act as expected	– test 4 & 5
▓ Check style and theme consistent, and to design	– test 4 & 5
▓ Check each sheet works as expected	– test 4 & 5
▓ Check all images load as expected	– test 4 & 5
▓ Check all animations load and work as expected	– test 4 & 5
▓ Check all sounds load and work as expected	– test 4 & 5

NB No data as such, as no input fields on website. Would include expected, extreme and erroneous data if relevant.

Part of the test data and expected results follow, showing that even for a system with no data, there are many navigational and visual aspects that also require checking. The first test for most systems would be to check that the menu and navigation around the system work – so forward and backward buttons take you where you expect to go, load up the correct screen and so on.

WW–hire website – Test data and expected results (extracts)		
Test number	**Test ref.**	**Test detail**
1		Html syntax checked for:
	1a	Index.html
	1b	Top.html
	1c	Etc.
	1d	Etc.
	1k	Tools.html
2		Virus check:
	2a	Index.html
	2b	Top.html
	2c	Etc.
	2d	Etc.
	2u	HH-welder.jpg
	2v	HH-paintspray.jpg
3		Initial load test. Check Top, Info and main:
	3a	In Internet Explorer
	3b	In Netscape
4		In Internet explorer
	4a	On Top, check sound file runs on load up
	4b	From Top (Menu), check Hand-held tools displays Hand page in rhs
	4c	Etc.
	4d	Etc.
	4s	– check bottomleft picture displays correct detail page
		– check click in enlarged picture returns to HH page
	4t	– check bottomright picture displays correct detail page
		– check click in enlarged picture returns to HH page
5		In Netscape Navigator
	5a	On Top, check sound file runs on load up
	5b	From Top (Menu), check Hand-held tools displays Hand page in rhs
	5c	Etc.
	5d	Etc.
	5s	– check bottomleft picture displays correct detail page
		– check click in enlarged picture returns to HH page
	5t	– check bottomright picture displays correct detail page
		– check click in enlarged picture returns to HH page

4.7 Test data/expected results

The nature of the test data should be such that:

- every step in the process is executed at least once
- the effectiveness of every area devoted to detecting invalid input is verified

- every route through the process, function or system is tried at least once
- the accuracy of the processing is verified (calculations checked, etc.)
- the system operates according to its original design specification.

To achieve these aims, you must be inventive in the design of the test data. Each test case must check something not tested by previous tests; there is no point in proving that a process which can successfully add a certain set of numbers can also add a similar set of numbers. The goal is to strain the system to its limit, and this is particularly important when it is to be used frequently by a number of different people.

Each input field that has validation must be checked with valid data, with invalid data and data at the extreme ends of any range.

For example, for a field with an allowable range of 1–20:

Test number	Field	Input	Expected result
1	xRange	4	Valid – moves to next input field
2	xRange	1	Valid – moves to next input field
3	xRange	20	Valid – moves to next input field
4	xRange	0	Invalid – error message displayed
5	xRange	21	Invalid – error message displayed
6	xRange	35	Invalid – error message displayed

- Test 1 is valid data
- Tests 2 and 3 are extreme data (either ends of the range)
- Tests 4 to 6 are invalid (or erroneous) data.

With many modern software packages, it is possible to restrict the input of fields by putting the allowable range or format checks into the package, by the use of restricted drop-down lists or restricted choices using radio buttons or check boxes. As long as these features are to be used and you have stated that this is so, then there is little need to construct endless tests for them. One reason for not using some of the in-built validation checks is that the error messages may not be very meaningful.

What does this mean?	
Automatic validation checks:	The software checks the data according to a set of rules. Be very careful with using such checks on some fields. For example, post codes have different shapes in different parts of the country – the following are all valid post codes in the UK: W8 5HN CH63 2QP LE2 3JQ

5 Implementation

Implementation is the manifestation of the detailed design you have carried out. Theoretically anyone should be able to take your specification and produce the functions and code and make all screens and reports exactly as you designed them.

In a business, implementation might be done by more than one person, or even more than one team at a time. Producing information systems is tricky and must be controlled and methodical to ensure that fully tested functionality is produced for the end user.

For the A2 project, the Implementation phase is worth 15 marks. The criteria for gaining those marks are shown below.

Maximum marks	Allocation of marks
11–15	■ The candidate has fully implemented the detailed design unaided, in an efficient manner and with no obvious defects. All the appropriate facilities of the software and hardware available were fully exploited. ■ The documentation is clear and thorough.
6–10	■ The candidate has implemented the essential elements of the design reasonably effectively and largely unaided. The implementation has exploited some of the relevant features of the software and hardware available. The documentation lacks detail or may have been omitted. ■ Alternatively, the candidate has fully implemented a simple design.
1–5	■ The design has been partially implemented. The implementation has exploited few relevant features of the software and hardware available. ■ The documentation lacks detail or may have been omitted.
0	■ There is no implementation.

Interpretation of implementation marks

Implementation (15)	11–15	6–10	1–5
Solution	Fully implemented, unaided	Essential elements implemented, largely unaided	Partial implementation
Appropriate techniques	Advanced techniques used, documentation complete	Some advanced techniques used, documentation poor	Few techniques used, documentation missing
Generic and package-specific skills	All appropriate facilities used	Some relevant facilities used	Few relevant facilities used
Hardware and software facilities	All appropriate facilities used	Some relevant facilities used	Few relevant facilities used

5.0 Solution

Appropriate data capture and data validation procedures must be used. The user interface must be consistent and professional – remember it is supposed to be for a business to use, not a group of 17-year-olds.

To gain high marks in a database project, there must be evidence of many features and functions being used – but most important is the fact that the solution must be relational. Three or four tables all used as separate entities will get no credit; at least one form and one report must be based on a query linking more than one table.

Make sure you have set up a relationship diagram and take a screen shot of it. All input fields must have validation designed into them. For any macros written, take a copy of the code. This section is all about evidence – someone just looking at the paper you produce must be able to see that the system works as stated.

Follow the design (otherwise marks will be lost). If, while implementing, you find changes to be made, either to improve an aspect or because something won't work the way it had been envisaged, make sure you keep a screen-dump trail of the old and new and make some notes. The point is to show that changes have been made in a controlled manner.

Tip for success:

Have a Word 'commentary/log' document open, so that screen dumps or notes can be added at any time.

In addition to everything else being produced, there must be a technical guide to the implementation – this should have lists of tables, screens, queries, report names and contents, how each macro is used/designed, the flow through the processes, any interdependencies, etc.

For the highest marks, you must have implemented your whole system, as designed, unless the system is so big that a partial implementation was planned at the start. If parts of it have not been implemented, then there must be commentary describing the problems encountered.

System documentation must be sufficient for someone else to come along and amend/update your system later.

5.1 Appropriate techniques

The appropriateness of the way your solution has been achieved will be assessed. Some advanced features of your chosen software must have been utilised. Simply using the package as any untrained person might use it to arrive at your solution is not enough – you have to prove that as a student of ICT for two years you know the capabilities and limitations of a range of software and can use it in the best possible way.

A list of advanced features is given for each package mentioned at the beginning of this unit. You should have had ample opportunity to investigate the package to be customised for your project so that you have been able to choose the best and most appropriate techniques to arrive at the optimum solution for your system.

Notes in your log will demonstrate how you used certain features and developed your solution, justifying why you chose one technique rather than another. An example for a database system is your choice about whether to merely link forms, or have a sub-form showing at the same time.

5.2 Generic and package-specific skills

This is an extension of the section above – you should prove you have package-specific skills by using the most appropriate features and function of the package, while also demonstrating that you are aware of all the generic features available.

Some of the simple generic skills include making sure everything is spell-checked, and that the screen showing to the user of your system is not cluttered with toolbars, status bars and so on. A user of a system is not interested in how it has been constructed, merely in how it works and does the job required. The users of the systems are not ICT experts – you are!

5.3 Hardware and software facilities

You should prove that you have used all hardware and software facilities in an appropriate manner.

Make sure all hardware use is logged – use of scanner, digital camera, printer or plotter, or any other input or output device. Storage and back-up devices could also be mentioned here.

As for software, you could provide proof of using back-up and restore facilities, different packages for test plan production, or project planning and control.

Make sure all use of hardware, such as scanners, is logged

If the target machine is different from the development machine, then somewhere there must be evidence that the system has been tried out on both machines.

6 Testing

The test plan is produced and marked as part of the design stage. Undertaking the testing, at a functional then at a system level, is what this section is about. Test data and results must show that every path through the system has been thoroughly tested, and every validation tried out with valid, erroneous and extreme data.

What does this mean?	
Extreme data:	Data that lies at each end of a condition. For example, if the range that is valid is 10 to 20, then test data for that field could look like this:

Value	Expected result	Actual result	Date tested/initials
2	Invalid		
9	Invalid		
10	Valid		
15	Valid		
20	Valid		
21	Invalid		
44	Invalid		

2, 9, 21 and 44 are erroneous tests
10 and 20 are extreme
15 is valid

The testing stage is worth 15 marks and the criteria for gaining the marks are shown below.

Maximum marks	Allocation of marks
11–15	■ The candidate has shown insight in demonstrating effective test data to cover most or all eventualities. There is a clear evidence of full end-user involvement in testing. The system works with a full range of test data (typical, extreme, erroneous); the test outputs are fully annotated.
6–10	■ The candidate has demonstrated a range of appropriate test data, perhaps with some assistance. There is evidence of end-user involvement during testing. The system works with a limited range of test data; the test outputs are annotated to a limited extent.
1–5	■ There is little evidence of testing. There has been only limited involvement of the end user in testing. It does not meet the design specification.
0	■ There is no evidence of testing.

Interpretation of testing marks

Implementation (15)	11–15	6–10	1–5
Strategy and plan	Insight shown in demonstrating effective testing to cover most or all eventualities	Range of appropriate tests, perhaps with assistance	Little evidence
Results of testing	System works to plan, test outputs fully annotated and cross-referenced to plan	System works with limited set of test data, some annotation	Little evidence, does not meet the design specification
Corrective action	Fully evident	Some evidence	Little evidence
End-user involvement	Fully evident	Some evidence	Little evidence

6.0 Strategy and plan

Unless this has changed significantly from that produced at the design stage, there is no need to include it here as well. It is often the case that some of the blanks can be filled in now – for example, who will perform the user testing and where will it be performed.

In real-life situations, often the users are assumed to be providing their own data, but when it comes to the point of user testing, it is found that they have not had time to prepare it, so they expect the developers to provide the data for them.

One way you can demonstrate that you have thought of this eventuality is to have some 'ideal' data prepared ready for your users – different from the data you have been testing with, as it is not necessary for the user to get bogged down in checking the validation on fields or any of the other detailed testing. They merely need to be able to find out whether the data they put in at the data input forms turns into the output they expect.

6.1 Results of testing

Make sure each test is evidenced with screen dumps and copies of printouts – and annotate (write hand notes on) each to cross-reference it to the test plan. Keep a log of testing: which test is done, the outcome, etc.

Set up an empty test log like the one in Figure 21 on the next page, and use it as you test. The test log will not be word-processed as it is a living document. Always use plenty of cross-references so that anyone coming after you can tell which test you completed, and can find the outcomes and the evidence associated with the test.

Task 4 – WW-hire – Test Log

Test Number	Test ref.	Date of test	Result	Comment	Further work or test
1					
	1a				
	1b				
	1c				
	1d				
	1e				
	1f				
	1g				
	1h				
	1j				
	1k				
2					
	2a				
	2b				
	2c				
	2d				
	2e				
	2f				
	2g				
	2h				
	2j				
	2k				
	2l				
	2m				
	2n				
	2p				

Figure 21

A sample test log

6.2 Corrective action

If there are any problems, make sure you screen dump any error messages. Any corrective action taken must be documented and evidenced to show that the problem has been solved.

Nothing works first time, and the examiners won't be impressed if it looks as though your project did. A couple of pieces of evidence of corrective action being taken go a long way towards a high mark for testing!

6.3 End-user involvement

Make sure that end users try out the system, if possible with their own live data, to see whether it works in a real situation. There must be evidence that the end user has been involved – a forged letter will be seen through easily!

7 User guide

A user guide will help to support the user in working with and understanding the system that has been developed. The guide is not supposed to be a training manual so it does not always need step-by-step instructions with sample data, but a 'How to …' section may be very useful for the first-time user.

The guide should be set out to reflect the knowledge and level of the user – for example, it should be a non-technical document for entry-level users who have little or no experience of working with computerised systems. For a more advanced user a more technical guide could be produced, outlining some of the more advanced features of the package you have used.

In all cases the use of jargon should be avoided and pictures and screen shots should be included to make the guide as user-friendly as possible.

Include installation instructions for your system, especially if it is the type of system that might be installed in many places. Even if you have already installed it on the target machine, you need to include start-up instructions, which may be to double-click an icon on the desktop. However, bear in mind that the software might have to move to a new machine, and in case of disaster users will need to know how to install the system.

A section in the guide should be for frequently asked questions, or a quick step-through guide. Another section that must be included is a trouble-shooting section – a 'What if' list.

Remember that the user guide is designed to be free-standing, so it should be a professional-looking document in its own right – with cover, contents page, headers, footers and page numbers (even if they are different in the content of the overall report).

When presenting the user guide, consider:

1 Varying the format. It does not necessarily have to be a set of A4 sheets – sometimes an A5 booklet looks better. If you are including a different size, ensure that it is firmly fixed to the rest of your work so it cannot get lost. Although in reality you may deliver the user guide electronically, on a CD for instance, for the purposes of this unit it must be printed out.

2 Printing the user guide in colour, if you have the facilities available, especially if your screen designs make use of colour. If you do have this facility available, and you design colour use to have meaning (e.g. having error messages in red), then you must be able to show that to the user. If that is the subject of a test condition, then you may also need to evidence it in testing.

Tip for success:

Most moderators (the examiners who look at your work) read the user guide first, to see what the system is supposed to do. This gives them the best overview of the system that they are going to look at. So do make sure it is attractive and easy to use.

The user guide is worth 8 marks. The criteria for gaining those marks are shown below.

Maximum marks	Allocation of marks
6–8	A comprehensive, well-illustrated user guide has been produced that deals with all aspects of the system (installation, back-up procedures, general use and trouble shooting).
4–5	An illustrated user guide has been produced that deals with general use of the system, but only vaguely considers other areas required to gain 6–8 marks.
1–3	A user guide has been produced that deals with general use of the system.
0	There is no user guide.

Interpretation of the user guide marks

User guide (8)	6–8	4–5	1–3
Functions of the system	All aspects covered, including installation, back-up, cyclical processes. Well illustrated.	General guide, not comprehensive. Illustrated.	A guide exists
Common problems	Comprehensive lists and answers	Vague or missing	Vague or missing
Appropriateness for the end user	Fully appropriate	Mostly appropriate, some technicalities	Not appropriate for end user, or not function based

7.0 Functions of the system

Every function must be covered – use plenty of screen dumps.

Make sure there is a contents page, and that this gives the functions of the system, not just screen by screen. Make the order logical, grouped by functional area – for example a section on how to maintain stock might include functions for 'Create new stock item', 'Amend stock description', 'Add stock', 'List stock'.

For each function, show the sequence of events if data is input – which screens will appear, which informational or error messages might be seen, etc.

When using screen dumps, make sure they can be read when printed out – no more than two or three per page, among text instructions. Follow a formula so that each page of instructions has a similar pattern. The reader will then know where to look for advice on, say, how to input a date of birth.

7.1 Common problems

The list of common problems will include not only functional problems that are specific to your system, but also any generic software or hardware problems that may occur. Common problems occur on starting software, on printing, and on saving.

While this does not need to be a comprehensive guide to software and hardware product, anticipation of the more common errors thrown up by operating systems will help the user to be successful with the system you have provided. This is especially important if one or more of your users is a novice computer user.

As part of this section, it is a good idea to add a 'Frequently asked questions' feature about the most common functions on the system. This will make the user's life easier.

7.2 Appropriateness for end user

The audience for the guide is a significant factor in how it is written. A technical guide, full of jargon, will serve only to confuse the novice user; alternatively, a user guide written in language suitable for a primary school pupil will only annoy the advanced technical user.

How do you get the balance right? The trick is to be helpful without being patronising.

If your users are all novice, make sure you spell out every step to be taken. Make instructions clear and simple, with pictures to illustrate each point, so they can see if they are doing things correctly. Try it out on someone who is a novice user and see what he or she says about the guide – which are the easy parts and which the complex. Add extra instructions or subtract items that are not helpful.

If your users are all advanced, you should be able to assume a starting level of competence. Construct your guide with that in mind, and ask someone at an equivalent level to try it out. Act on their suggestions about where you need extra information and where there is too much information.

If you have a mixture of users, include the step-by-step guide for novices and also a shortened, or quick-start, section for the more advanced who will be able to use the system more intuitively.

If your system has been designed well, helpful messages and sensibly named buttons, fields and so on should make learning the new package easier.

8 Evaluation

Evaluation is not about patting yourself on the back, but is an occasion to be fully critical of what has been produced. It carries 10 marks.

The purpose is to assess the effectiveness of the solution in relation to the original requirements specification. If you made a good performance criteria list in the specification, then evaluation should be fairly easy. Go through each item in turn saying how you met or failed to meet that criterion.

Evaluation is all about assessing what was successful and how your solution could be improved. Look at your original objectives. Make a note of those you achieved and those that weren't achieved. You'll need to look at your testing to find evidence that you fulfilled these objectives. Make a note of where you show the evidence.

Try to evaluate why some objectives weren't achieved, and make notes on why not. You don't need to know a final solution, but try to explain how your attempted solutions failed. Be honest!

Make sure you include an end-user questionnaire. Your end users are the only people who can truly evaluate the system. Ask them to complete a summary evaluation (cross-referenced to their original requirements list) printed or written on company notepaper. A simple letter praising your efforts is not sufficient.

The evaluation is worth 10 marks. The criteria for gaining those marks are shown below.

Maximum marks	Allocation of marks
9–10	■ The candidate has considered clearly a full range of qualitative and quantitative criteria for evaluating the solution. The candidate has fully evaluated his/her solution intelligently against the requirements of the user(s). Evidence of end-user involvement during this stage has been provided.
6–8	■ The candidate has discussed a range of relevant criteria for evaluating the solution. The candidate has evaluated his/her solution against the requirements of the user(s) in most respects. Some, but not all, performance indicators have been identified. Any modifications to meet possible major limitations and/or enhancements have been specified, maybe with assistance.
3–5	■ The system has only been partially evaluated against the original specification and the requirements of the user(s). This may be because the original specification was poor. Few, if any, performance indicators have been identified. Discussion concerning the limitations or enhancements to the system have largely been omitted or have required some prompting.
1–2	■ Little attempt at evaluation has been made. No performance indicators have been identified. Discussion concerning the limitations or enhancements to the system have been omitted or are limited and have required considerable prompting.
0	■ No attempt at evaluation has been made.

Interpretation of evaluation marks

Evaluation (10)	9–10	6–8	3–5	1–2
Assessment	Fully evaluated against user requirements	Mostly evaluated against user requirements	Partially evaluated against user requirements	Little evaluation attempted
Awareness of criteria	Fully evaluated against performance criteria	Range of criteria used for evaluation	Few performance indicators identified	No performance indicators identified
Limitations	Fully discussed	Some discussion	Little or no discussion	Little or no discussion
End-user involvement	Full evidence	Some evidence	Little or no evidence	Little or no evidence

8.0 Assessment

The easiest way to get the top marks available here is to take each of the user requirements listed in the analysis (the list of what they wanted – a list of stock, a re-order stock function, etc.) and address each one in turn – stating whether your implemented system now provides that requirement in full, or in part, stating what if any adjustments were made, and how it is fulfilled. You could give a function reference and say how you get to it in the system.

8.1 Awareness of criteria

The list of criteria is the one produced in the analysis that has the qualitative and quantitative items – so it is more than merely the user's functional requirements list.

Performance criteria can often be subjective, so you definitely need a third party to evaluate your system. Ideally this will be a selection of people including your end user. A questionnaire about the whole of your system would help you.

8.2 Limitations

You need to be objective in your evaluation of your system. It is time to be honest.

- What could have been done better?
- Were the limitations that you identified the fault of the design, of the limitations of your knowledge, or of the hardware or the software?
- What improvements could have been incorporated?
- What future improvements could be made?
- What would you have done differently if you had had the time?

An example (for the website used earlier) follows.

Limitations and improvements

Problems encountered

- The CSE validator changed the case of characters in the filename so that the case was different between source code and filename held. This does not seem to matter to Windows/DOS, but has serious effects once on the stair server. Most of the errors encountered on testing were due to this problem.
- The site worked as expected within Internet Explorer; however, on Netscape Navigator there were many problems, starting with the browser not recognising the Index file. In the end, I put Top (frame) in one window, and used that to test the other 3 pages, each loading into the same second window.
- The Internal workings on Main were fine.
- On Hand-Held page, all was OK, apart from when loading the larger pictures. They were not aligned correctly (yet all text was).
- On Plant Tools page, the second internal hyperlink did not work – a case mismatch problem.
- On all pages in Netscape, the font was not displaying correctly, probably due to a shorter font list on the browser.

Improvements

- Need to design in filename cases/capitalisation and be consistent one way or the other (need to experiment with changes).
- Need to amend so that it works in Netscape properly (i.e. in frames).
- Need to find a font that suits all browsers.
- Need to reduce font and picture size in places, especially Info page, to reduce the amount of scrolling – at the moment the 'Contact us' link is out of sight.
- Main page – possibly lighten some of the background colour.
- A different design might make it more friendly – maybe have thumbnails for larger machinery with detail pages, as on Hand-Held page – this would mean that 'Special offers' would be on view.
- Plant Page – correct the mistake, so links work better; also needs font changes and formatting amendments as mostly <pre> text.
- Drill, Buffer, Welder and Paintspray pages need amending to ensure the picture is centred – investigate putting in a one-cell table if won't work as a free image.
- Could add a visitor counter.
- Logo used needs redesigning for this company to fit in with overall design.
- Monitor visitors and e-mails to see if it is worth considering offering on-line equipment booking as a way to expand the business.

8.3 End-user involvement

Questionnaires and meeting notes are needed here. You need to have concrete evidence that your end user has been involved at more than just the start and the end – so testing logs, meeting notes, mentions in your development log are all useful as evidence.

Use the sign-off log shown on page 155. Ask your users to write a letter of acceptance, evaluating your system and its usefulness to them.

9 Project report

The project report brings together all the work that you have produced during development of your system. This should be usable as a 'handover pack' for a technical person taking on the maintenance of your system. It should therefore contain details of analysis, design, code, test plans and data, expected results, any tips and tricks. In short, it includes all the technical documentation that has arisen plus the running commentary of how you did it, with annotations.

The whole report must be presented logically, with a cover and contents list, indexed if you have time, and page numbered from front to back. Even if individual sections (e.g. the user guide) already have page numbers, the whole report needs numbering, so that the contents page at the front is accurate. Do this page numbering as your very last task, then complete your contents page, put on your front page and tag the whole package together.

Moderators want the project report to be presented with punched holes and kept together with treasury tags that are long enough for them to turn over the pages without danger of pages being ripped. Never put pages into plastic wallets, or bind them – this often leads to pages being lost or ripped. Lever arch files and plastic wallets merely add to the cost and the bulk. Dividers (even pieces of coloured paper showing a section title) between sections are good signposts for the marker and moderator.

There are 8 marks available for the report, so it is worth taking a bit of care, as they are easy marks to gain. The criteria for gaining the marks are shown below.

Maximum marks	Allocation of marks
7–8	■ A well-written, fully illustrated and organised report has been produced. It describes the project accurately and concisely.
5–6	■ A well-written report has been produced, but lacks good organisation. Alternatively a well-organised report has been produced which is of limited quality.
3–4	■ The report is of generally poor quality but shows some evidence of organisation. There have been a number of deficiencies and omissions.
1–2	■ The report has been poorly organised and presented with few or no diagrams. There have been a considerable number of omissions.
0	■ No report is present.

Interpretation of report stage marks

Project report (8)	7–8	5–6	3–4	1–2
Title and contents, headers, footers and page numbers	Fully organised	Lacks good organisation	Some organisation	Poor organisation
General	Well-written, fully illustrated, describes project accurately and concisely	Well-written, of limited quality	Poor quality, with deficiencies and omissions	Few or no diagrams, many omissions

9.0 Title, contents, headers, footers, page numbers

Make sure that all of these are present. The footer should give your name, candidate number, centre name and centre number on every page. The name of the system should feature most on the header. For example, the user guide should look like the professional document it is supposed to be – and the header should say it is the user guide. For the rest of the report, the header should consist of the system name and the section.

Figure 22

Constructing a header

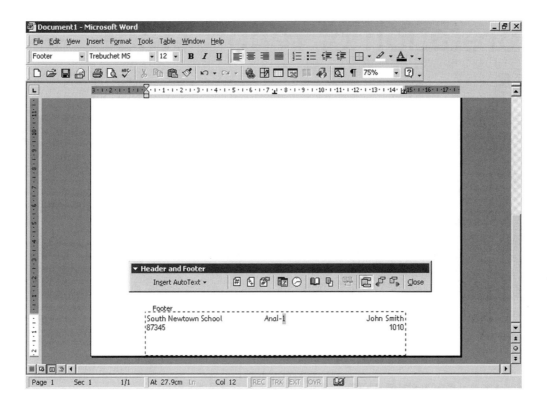

Figure 23
Constructing a footer

9.1 General

All sections should be organised logically. Anything that is used in more than one section should be cross-referenced properly. For example, the test plan may be in the design section, but be referenced in the testing section.

All diagrams should be given a title and referenced – a list of diagrams could be included, indicating title and page number. This list would be placed after the contents page.

Check your report carefully before you hand it in. Make sure all spelling mistakes are corrected, and that the grammar is suitable for your audience – do not use terms your audience is unlikely to understand. Do this verification before you add page numbers, perhaps asking someone to read your work and make comments. You could do this section by section so that it is not left to the end, when you may be in a rush to complete your project.

These report marks are easy ones to pick up. If you have worked in a professional manner throughout your project, you will have little difficulty putting your report together with enough organisation to get maximum marks.

REVISION

This revision unit looks at topics that are covered in the A2 specification and, using past papers and mark schemes, addresses how the knowledge gained in the A2 study modules can be applied to the examination questions.

The two A2 theory papers are synoptic, which means that answers can be drawn from all areas of the specification, including the knowledge gained by producing both the task solution work for AS Unit 3 and the project for A2 Unit 6. It is expected that these two papers will be taken at the end of two years of study of ICT, and the standard is set at that level. Everyday knowledge will often not be enough to gain any marks – you need to use precise technical terminology and give answers showing an underlying understanding of the subject.

These two papers also always have an essay or extended question as the last one on the paper. Each is worth 20 marks, out of the 90 available per paper. You therefore need to approach the essay questions carefully to maximise your marks.

Reading and understanding the question is half the battle for marks. If you just glance at a question, see a technical term, and – feeling relieved to recognise something – simply write everything you know about that term, you will be disappointed when the results are published. Accurate use of technical language, and using the correct term in the correct context, becomes more important at A2 level.

Specifically, this revision unit covers:

- Examination vocabulary: the words and what they are asking you to do
- Examination technique: how to read the question and interpret what is required
- Essay writing, structure and planning: gaining the 'quality of written communication' marks
- Frequently asked definitions: technical vocabulary
- Lists to use for quick topic revision.

1 **Examination vocabulary**

One of the most important factors in exam success is learning to read the question paper. You need to be familiar with the vocabulary used. Most questions on the A2 papers, as on the AS papers, are formatted so that there is a question stem, giving some form of context to the information required. This may set the context in a shop, a bank, a factory or a particular office or school.

This stem is followed by one or more questions that normally start with a key word and give the number of items required. The items must be correct for the context given, so be careful to read the stem properly.

Key word(s)	Normal mark allocation per point	Comments
State, identify *or* name	1	Answer with one word or a short phrase for each point. Writing a paragraph won't gain any more than the one mark available, so be precise!
Give	1	As above, but sometimes more than a single word is needed to make the meaning clear. Often used in questions such as 'give one advantage and one disadvantage …'
Define	1 or 2	This is normally asked of a technical term, and a sentence would usually be enough.
Describe	2	This normally needs you to name something plus give a description for 2 marks; sometimes the question says 'name and describe'.
Explain	2 or 3	Similar to *describe*, but needing a different slant. Remember to keep the explanation in context and watch out for the number of marks per point made.
Using an example	1	This will normally add 1 mark to each *describe* or *explain* answer.
With the aid of an example	perhaps 1	This quite often means that 1 of the marks of a *describe* or *explain* is specifically for the example.

Sample questions

The key words described above are used in the following ways:

- **Give** three characteristics of good information, **with an example** for each.
- **Define** *formal information*.
- **Explain** what is meant by approval to proceed.
- **Describe** three ways of giving user support.

2 Examination technique

First make sure you have at least two blue or black pens and a pencil when you go into the examination room.

The examinations are 2 hours long, which is plenty of time for most people to answer all the questions carefully. It gives enough time to read through the paper before you start. Some tips:

- Decide which topic is being examined, and make a quick note beside the question, or make notes on the back page of your answer booklet to remind yourself; you can simply cross through this later to indicate it was rough work.
- Make sure you check the back of the paper – it has been known for candidates to miss the last question because they did not turn over the page!
- As the essay question is worth 20 of the 90 marks, allow enough time to plan and write it – a minimum of 20 minutes, but aim to have 30 minutes available.
- Take a deep breath and begin. Once the first couple of questions have been done, you should begin to relax.

Examiners prefer the questions to be attempted in the order they are set out on the paper. There are normally around 10 questions, the first one or two of which are always very straightforward, to ease into the paper – they tend to ask for short definitions or are simple *state* or *name* questions. Look over past papers and answer schemes to familiarise yourself with the styles of questions. They are freely available on the AQA website (www.aqa.org.uk).

An answer booklet, normally with 16 blank pages, is provided – only those with large writing will need to use a continuation sheet. You can therefore afford to spread out the answers. Leave space at the end of every question, in case you want to add anything later. If the previous question ends in the last third of a page, start the next question on a new page – it is not necessary to try to fit all the answers into the smallest possible number of pages!

Make sure you read the stem of the question at least once, so that you fully understand the context. Read all parts to a question and decide exactly what information is being asked for in each part. They are usually related in some way, so don't write down all known facts in part a, and then feel at a loss for more when you come to part c. Next, look at the question word, as described above, and the number of marks allocated, and plan the answer accordingly – if there are three points for a question, there need to be three parts to the answer (see the examples on the next page).

2.0 Some points to remember

- Make sure that an example is included if specifically asked for.
- If two marks are available, find two phrases to write (extend your first thoughts and be explicit); if there are three, then find three phrases.
- Keep referring back to the stem and keep the answer in the context given, if there is one – writing about supermarkets when the given context is a medical centre will mean you lose marks.
- Don't just write down all the information you can remember about a topic. If four items were requested and the first four you write down do not get the marks, the examiner may not read any further in a long list.
- Don't write a paragraph if the question word was *state* or *give* – it is a waste of time and energy and does not gain any more marks.
- Don't write a single word or phrase if the question word is *describe* or *explain*.

189

2.1 Sample answers

Here are some example answers using the guidelines above. Note the differences in answer style where more marks are on offer for each point made.

Question:
State **four** factors that will need managing in a period of change. *(4 marks)*

Answer:
1 Organisational structure
2 Re-skilling of the workforce
3 Attitude
4 Internal procedures.

Question:
Describe **four** factors that will need managing in a period of change. *(8 marks)*

Answer:
1 The structure of the organisation may need adjustments to take account of the improved information flow following the introduction of a new IS. De-layering may occur as there may be less need for manual management of organisational information.
2 Re-skilling of the workforce will be necessary to ensure that all employees, whether higher management, middle management or at production level, are able to use the new IS to its full potential.
3 Staff attitude is another factor that may need managing. Some may fear job loss, some may feel they are being de-skilled. It is important to keep staff informed and involved throughout the period of change so that they can embrace the new IS, and see it in a positive light, not a negative one.
4 With a new IS, procedures will change to take account of the input needs and outputs from the new system. The improved information flow should create a more efficient organisation that will make working life more satisfying for all users at every level.

Question:
State **three** methods of training. *(3 marks)*

Answer:
1 External training course
2 Computer-based training
3 Paper-based training manual.

Question:
Describe **three** methods of training for a receptionist, saying why each is suitable. *(9 marks)*

Answer:
1 One possibility is to send the receptionist on an external course where a qualified expert will show a class of students how to use the system, normally a mixture of book study and hands-on practice. Here, the receptionist would be able to ask questions and collaborate with other students, which can boost confidence.
2 Computer-based training is an option. This would normally come in the form of a CD-ROM which has a set route through a series of topics in a logical format. Often a technique is demonstrated in multi-media form, followed by an opportunity to practise with some set exercises. Finally, there is usually a 'test' on each topic that has to be passed before going on to the next topic, to ensure steady progress. It is suitable as the receptionist could use this at a time of day to suit himself or herself, rather than at an externally set time, and sections can be repeated until confidence is gained.

3 Paper-based training manuals normally contain chapters with step-by-step instructions on how to use a particular feature or function of a system. There are normally illustrations demonstrating what should happen when particular steps are carried out. There are often additional features such as a trouble-shooting section or a 'Frequently asked questions' section. This could be suitable for the receptionist as it can be consulted away from the computer, for preparation or recap purposes.

3 The essay question

On each of the A2 papers, there is an essay or extended question worth 20 marks. This is a considerable portion of the 90 marks available, so it should be approached in an organised and positive way.

If possible, allow between 30 and 45 minutes to answer the essay question. Preparation time is a necessity for this question, to maximise your marks.

A concise two to three pages of the answer booklet, in well-written and well-organised prose that covers all the topics signposted, should gain at least 15 marks. Waffle and repetition are to be avoided.

The 20 marks are split into 16 marks for content (what is written) and 4 marks for quality of written communication (how it is written).

3.0 Content

Usually the essay question is written as a statement or quotation, followed by a directive (often *discuss*) and a set of bullet points (normally three or four). Where there are bullet points, the content marks are normally distributed evenly between them, so they should all be covered to ensure maximum marks.

Use the essay-planning techniques that you learnt at GCSE level (notes, spider diagrams, mind maps, etc.). Use the answer booklet to write a plan which shows the topics to be included in the answer. Try to arrange this in a logical order, but spend no more than 10 minutes on it.

Once you are happy with the plan (you can always add to it if something else occurs to you while you are writing), start on the essay. Do not write out the question – it does not gain any marks; however, a good introduction can sometimes bring up valuable points that do not need to be repeated later.

Keep the answer in a logical order. Follow the bullet point order if possible, to make it easy for the examiner to mark the work. Do not spend too long on the first bullet point at the expense of the last one or two – marks are usually awarded evenly over the bullet points.

Try to keep the content logically organised. Make sure each paragraph is about a particular point (do not skip between topics in mid-sentence) and signpost changes in topic with phrases such as 'the implications of … are …', 'some problems that might be encountered are …'). Write an introduction and a conclusion that do not repeat all the points made. Opinions are sometimes asked for, so make sure they are included if required.

If the five-minute warning is given and the essay is only half-complete, it may be wise to bullet point all the rest of your topics, so that the examiner can see the order of content you intended. This will cost you marks for 'quality of written communication', but may gain more content marks.

The only way to improve essay-writing skills is to practise, practise, practise.

3.1 Quality of written communication

Four marks are available for quality of written communication. The official guide to examiners is as follows.

- To gain three or four marks, the essay must be in prose and with fairly good grammar, punctuation and spelling (occasional lapses are overlooked).
- Most students should be capable of gaining three marks, if they have gained a 'C' at GCSE English Language.
- Paragraphs must be used.
- Handwriting must be legible.

4 marks	The candidate has expressed complex ideas clearly and fluently. Sentences and paragraphs follow on from one another smoothly and logically. Arguments will be consistently relevant and well structured. There will be few, if any, errors of grammar, punctuation and spelling.
3 marks	The candidate has expressed moderately complex ideas clearly and reasonably fluently through well-linked sentences and paragraphs. Arguments will be generally relevant and well structured. There may be occasional errors of grammar, punctuation and spelling.
2 marks	The candidate has expressed straightforward ideas clearly, if not always fluently. Sentences and paragraphs may not always be well connected. Arguments may sometimes stray from the point or be weakly presented. There may be some errors of grammar, punctuation and spelling, but not such as to suggest a weakness in these areas.
1 mark	The candidate has expressed simple ideas clearly, but may be imprecise and awkward in dealing with complex or subtle concepts. Arguments may be of doubtful relevance or obscurely presented. Errors in grammar, punctuation and spelling may be noticeable and intrusive, suggesting weaknesses in these areas.

4 Technical vocabulary

Some questions come up time after time on the A2 papers, requiring basic definitions of terms. These are easy marks to earn, so make sure you learn and understand the necessary terms. Knowing these should enable you to reach the pass (E) grade – further application of knowledge and understanding separates the Es, Cs and As.

4.0 ICT 4

Term	Acceptable definition
Agreed deliverables	Users' requirements are met with documents at specific stages and a system that has agreed content is produced to agreed standards.
Application audit trail	Used to track what has happened – it could be recorded before and after each transaction. Normally a user ID and timing information are included, plus any value changes. It is done so that lost data or information can be recovered; also to track unauthorised use of an application, especially in financial systems of all kinds.
Approval to proceed	To ensure the users are satisfied with work to date, they are asked to sign off a stage, giving the go-ahead for the project to continue.
Audit software	Using packages that can be bought, or bespoke systems, audit software tracks and checks transactions and events, especially in accounting-type applications. This is a different application of audit software from that used to track machine or network usage.
Clear timescales	So that the project can be monitored, stage-end dates or deadlines are set which are achievable and which both parties have agreed to.
Code of conduct	A set of procedures and rules of behaviour; how a professional person should conduct himself or herself within an industry, including ethical considerations.
Code of practice	A set of rules which governs the use of ICT systems, set out by an organisation to be followed by employees. It may refer to the responsibilities of employees and set out penalties. It is separate from any legal or ethical (code of conduct) responsibilities.
Data accuracy	Gathered data can easily be inaccurate, so it should be subject to verification and validation checks; it needs checking regularly against the data source and updating if necessary. Data accuracy also pertains to grading systems – e.g. with exam results, if a mark between 30 and 45 is a grade C, and only the 'C' is held, the exact mark is not known so the data it is not as accurate as it could be.
Data capture	The process of gathering data into a system for processing. It could be captured on paper forms, then manually keyed; stored as a file on disk; or sent as an e-mail attachment.
Data capture method	Different methods studied in AS Unit 2 include bar-code scanning, keyboarding, OCR, OMR, MICR, swipe-card reading, etc.

Term	Acceptable definition
Data processing system	Precise, low level, electronic data capture is used for repetitive or routine business activities. Also known as transaction processing systems.
Data transcription	Inputting, normally from a hand-written or typed format, of data into a capturing system. For example, a mail-order form has to have the details keyed into the ordering system (usually the same one is filled in on-screen by the call-centre staff as is filled in on-line for the web-based system).
Data translation	Data may be gathered in one form or format but be translated into a different form or format to be input to a system. Normally some form of translation table is used when, for example, amalgamating meter reading systems. The codes used are not the same, so software translates one set to agree with the other.
Development life-cycle of an IS	Stages of the life-cycle, in the waterfall method, are feasibility study; systems analysis (also known as requirements analysis then logical design); design (also known as physical or detailed design); build and unit test (also known as implementation); functional testing (also known as system testing or alpha testing); user testing (also known as beta testing); implementation (also known as installation); review; on-going maintenance.
Effective presentation	Information must be presented in a way that is suitable for the task – and the person using it. There would be no point in giving a managing director a detailed list of all transactions taking place at a particular point of sale – decision-makers need grouping, rationalisation and interpretation of information based on pre-agreed rules.
External information needs	Information that external agencies might need. Suppliers need ordering information from an organisation; exam boards need student details from a school or college; the Inland Revenue needs details of tax paid from an employer.
External source	Information or data may come from an outside agency. Tax and National Insurance bands and rates are set by central government and input into payroll systems; names and addresses may be bought for marketing purposes.
Formal information flow	A system with fully documented and agreed procedures, stating stages of flow control, exception handling and distribution.
Formal methods for developing an information system (you need to be aware that these exist, but not to be able to describe them)	The traditional waterfall life-cycle (as described above); rapid application development methods (RAD, DSDM – divide the project into sections and develop and implement each in turn, rather than waiting until all is done before implementation); object-oriented methods (where some data or an event is the object – used in VB-style point-and-click systems).

Term	Acceptable definition
Implementation-level task	Also known as tactical level. Normally middle management – day-to-day or short-term management activities.
Industry standard package	Off-the-retail-shelf package such as MS Office XP; Sage Accounts; Lotus Notes – in fact anything that is used in many small to medium businesses.
Informal information flow	Information that naturally arises, such as in a phone call or personal conversation, during a meeting or by observation.
Information system	A collection of data processed to improve performance or used as an aid to decision-making or support for management.
Internal information needs	Information which the business requires to function effectively.
Internal source	Information arising from an internal system as input to another, or from a data-gathering exercise that is part of the organisation's portfolio of operations. For example, in a supermarket, information from the point-of-sale system is used as input to a sales MIS system.
Levels of management	Higher – strategic; middle – tactical; lower – operational. Information needs to be at the right level for the task.
Management information system (MIS)	A system to convert data from internal and external sources into information, communicated in an appropriate form so that managers at different levels of an organisation can use the information produced to enable them to make effective decisions.
Operational-level task	Repetitive, continuous, hour-to-hour activities – e.g. stocking shelves in a supermarket.
Risk analysis	Identifying each element of a successful information system, placing a value (to the business) on that element, identifying any potential threats to that element, and the likelihood of the threat occurring.
Strategic-level task	Assisting higher (board-level) management in deciding where to take the business.
Tactical-level task	Assisting middle management to make mid-term decisions for a department or branch of an organisation.
Value of information in decision-making	Information must be relevant, accurate, up to date, etc. so that the right decisions are made with the best information available.

4.1 **ICT 5**

Term	Acceptable definition
Addressing mechanism	Having a unique address so that source and destination devices can be identified on a network or the World Wide Web. Communication can then be sent to the required recipient.
Alpha testing	Testing performed in-house by the developer of the software, using a fixed set of data to generate predicted results, to ensure that each part of the solution does what it is supposed to do.
Back-up options	There is a long list in AS Unit 2 – frequency, what gets backed up, the media used, etc. This unit requires you to think about what is suitable for each situation.
Back-up scheduling	The timing of the back-up – daily back-up is useless on a real-time system for live data. Allow time in the daily run schedule for back-ups to take place.
Back-up storage	Suitability is the key – is a RAID system really necessary? A fire-proof safe is OK for fires, but there should be copies off-site.
Beta testing	Performed by a select set of end users outside the development team or organisation, using data that may not have been considered by the developers ('live' data), to ensure the solution works in real situations. End users can provide feedback to the developers.
Client/server database	Where the data is held on the server and the client (or attached computer) requests the data from the server, which supplies it.
Configuration	The total platform on which the organisation operates its ICT systems – the network, the hardware, and the systems software, including operating system(s).
Data consistency	Normalising data means that the same data is not held more than once, so a change to the data results in all functions using the changed value.
Data distribution	Data is held in different places – e.g. in a bank, head office has a full copy of all the data, but each branch downloads its local account information each morning and works on the local copy of the data all day, uploading the local data to update the master copy in the evening.
Data independence	Previously, if the structure of a file was changed (a new field was added, for instance) every program that used that file had to be changed, costing time and money. With an RDBMS (see the next page) each program only states the fields it will be using, so changes to the location of that field in the structure do not affect the programs. The data is independent of the programs – also known as program-data independence.
Data integrity	An RDBMS is designed so that related data stays related – no data is lost through bad links. Unique identifying fields or keys are used on each set of data (entity).

Term	Acceptable definition
Data redundancy	If data is repeated unnecessarily (i.e. not for reasons of having a link field), space is wasted – this is called redundancy.
Database administrator	An administrator's responsibilities include monitoring performance of the RDBMS; notifying users of changes made; allocating user access; providing training to users; back-up procedures; making data dictionary changes. In small businesses he or she may also take on the role of database designer.
Database designer	A highly technical and skilled role in large organisations. The designer takes a logical system design and applies it using the RDBMS to create a fully normalised and functional database system, with all rules and procedures in place.
(Relational) database management system – (R)DBMS	A collection of programs that allows manipulation of data, and the definition of a data dictionary, and where the data is stored in tables that are related through linked fields. It provides a buffer between the user and the data, controlling access and providing consistent view to levels of users.
De facto standards	Standards that happen (or arise) as a result of market success (e.g. MS-Windows over Mac OS), and through popular choice; you are not legally bound to adhere, but common sense says if you don't you won't sell any of your products! More formal standards are 'de jure' standards, set by professional bodies for the industry. They include voltage and so on in different countries.
Emulation hardware	Equipment that is attached to an existing system to make it appear to be on a different platform (e.g. a video card that emulates a different graphics capability).
Emulation software	Software that makes programs perform on a non-compatible system as they would on a compatible one, e.g. allowing software to read file types that would not normally be readable.
Entity relationships	Entities (stores of related data, like files in old terminology) are related in an RDBMS. Relationships are one-to-one, one-to-many, many-to-one or many-to-many. Each child has one mother; each order has many items; each item can be bought from many suppliers; many GCSE grades can be earned by many students.
Evaluation criteria	Indicators that are important to this system. Normally there are added weightings to prioritise the items.
Evaluation of software	If investing in a new system, there is a two-fold evaluation or decision-making process. First, how to buy (in-house, etc.), then if a package, comparisons. The procedure is to pin down requirements, generate a list of criteria, gather data and weight and evaluate, produce a report, then decide.
Evaluation report	Findings from the evaluation. Content includes methodology used; actual evaluation; recommendation; justification for the recommendation.

Term	Acceptable definition
Human/computer interaction	The human factors, including user-friendliness; help for novices; shortcuts for experts; and maximising efficiency by making use of human long-term memory.
Human/computer interface	Command-driven, menu-driven, and graphical user interface, as listed in AS Unit 2. Factors such as consistency of screen design, use of colour, meaningful icons, layout consistency with data capture form, built-in demonstrations, help keys, function keys that do the same thing throughout systems, and meaningful error messages are important.
Information management policy	An overriding statement of how the organisation approaches the storage and processing of its data and information, including the hardware and software platform to be used throughout the company. It may make a statement about using Microsoft products and upgrading every 12 months; it may state that all machines must have a certain amount of RAM or processor power, and so on.
Maintenance releases	The developer releases corrected versions of the software or functionality that has been added to the original system or package. Sometimes, developments are deliberately phased (especially with rapid development methods) so that functionality is available a little at a time and improvements are supplied with some new functionality.
Network accounting	Accounting software records usage in terms of who, what, when and for how long, for the purpose of charging for CPU use or application use. This is often done in large organisations for budgeting purposes.
Network audit	Monitoring who logs on, when and where, what applications they use, what sites they visit (on the Internet) and so on – mainly for ensuring safety and following procedures.
Network environments	Choice of network environment affects the user interface, and what users can and cannot see – security procedures, control over software, control over files and data, access rights and so on. Network strategy differs from organisation to organisation, according to differing needs and where the equipment is sited. Network clients in public places will be subject to stricter security than those in a single office site.
Network security	Using a secure operating system to provide log-in and password system, access rights, and safety of software and data held on the network. Measures to prevent unlawful access are covered in AS units 1 and 2 – physical, procedural, software-based, encryption and so on.
Normalisation	The concept of breaking down complex data structures into simpler forms. 1NF removes repeating data; 2NF removes partial-key dependencies; 3NF removes non-key dependencies.
Protocols and standards	Rules that define how network devices communicate. This provides portability of data across a wide range of hardware, software and file types. Many protocols exist for various types of hardware, and communications systems and networks. World Wide Web examples are – IP, TCP and HTTP.
URL	Universal Resource Locator – an easy-to-understand mechanism for addresses on the World Wide Web.

5 Quick topic revision

Sometimes it is useful to recap what is included in a topic area, especially in those areas where exam questions often ask for lists or descriptions, such as 'describe four' or 'give three'.

The lists below can act as an aide-memoir. They could be used for testing yourself or working with a friend to test each other; they could also be used as a class exercise during the revision period, with the teacher asking for items, or a verbal expansion of one item on a list. Alternatively, the lists could be used as a basis for a team quiz, where the same questions are asked of all.

5.0 ICT 4 topics

- **Factors influencing success or failure of an IS:**
  - inadequate analysis
  - inappropriate or excessive management demands
  - emphasis on computer system
  - concentration on low-level data processing, not on information needs
  - lack of professional standards
  - lack of management knowledge about capabilities of ICT and systems
  - lack of management involvement in design.
- **Factors influencing an IS in an organisation:**
  - general organisational structure
  - planning and decision-making methods
  - legal and audit requirements
  - management organisation and functions
  - information flow
  - responsibility for the IS within an organisation
  - hardware and software
  - behavioural factors (personality, motivation, adaptability)
  - standards.
- **Characteristics of information:**
  - source – internal, external, primary, secondary
  - nature – quantitative, qualitative, formal, informal
  - level – strategic, tactical, operational
  - time span – historical, current, future
  - frequency (of collection/production) – real-time, hourly, daily, monthly, etc.
  - use – for planning, control, decision-making
  - form – written, visual, aural, sensory
  - type – disaggregated (i.e. separate/itemised), aggregated (i.e. grouped), sampled.
- **Good information and delivery are:**
  - relevant
  - accurate
  - complete
  - to the right person
  - at the right time

- in the right detail
- promoting user confidence
- understandable
- via correct channels of communication.

Factors that must be managed when change occurs:
- People
  - their attitude to change
  - possible re-skilling
  - training issues
  - employment pattern and condition changes
- Organisational
  - appropriate levels of management
  - right information to right person
  - information strategy, codes of practice
  - internal procedures/standards
- Other
  - security procedures
  - compliance with legislation (heath and safety, data protection, computer misuse, software copyright)
  - ability to cope with legislative changes (e.g. tax rule changes may mean payroll systems need amending)
  - interfaces with external suppliers, purchasers or other external bodies.

Why have a corporate information security policy and what does it cover?
- prevention of misuse
- misuse detection
- investigation into possible misuse
- checks that procedures are being followed
- identification of staff responsibilities
- agreeing disciplinary procedures.

Threats to information systems:
- physical security breaches
- document security lapses
- personnel security
- hardware security
- communications security
- software security.

Factors in disaster contingency planning:
- scale/size of organisation
- timing (how important is it to recover immediately?)
- costs of plan (external contract needed?)
- likelihood of disaster happening.

Methods of enforcing and controlling data protection legislation:
- departmental data protection officer in place
- detailed job descriptions
- procedures to follow up anomalies
- security – password/physical/log-ins/firewalls/encryption

- strict code of practice on personal databases/software, etc.
- education of staff
- network activity logging
- use of access levels
- disciplinary procedures.

Methods of enforcing and controlling software misuse legislation:

- not allowing installation of unauthorised/unlicensed software
- not allowing copying of software for home/unlicensed use
- corporate hardware/software policy
- virus scanning of any externally supplied disk
- detailed job descriptions
- separation of duties so that no one has control of the complete job
- regular audits of software on all computers/network
- central control of licensing (either by a person or by software monitoring)
- monitoring of Internet usage/downloading
- disciplinary procedures.

Methods of enforcing and controlling health and safety legislation:

- health and safety officer to control practices
- regular inspections of workstations against health and safety criteria (electrical equipment, VDU emissions, etc.)
- regular inspections of workstations against ergonomic criteria (seat positioning, wrist supports, sight levels, etc.)
- staff training on health and safety legislation when working with computers and especially VDUs
- design and thorough testing of software
- procedures for ensuring faulty equipment is replaced in a timely manner
- written procedures/memos/posters advising on good health and safety practice
- disciplinary procedures.

User support options:

- Industry standard:
  - existing user base user groups
  - support articles/newsletters
  - supplied utilities (or downloadable)
  - specialist bulletin boards
  - Internet site information
  - e-mail systems for information/enquiry
- Software house:
  - help desk/phone line
  - on-site technical support
  - help system included with package
  - user guides/other documentation
  - communication systems as above.

Training options:

- CBT
- classroom – in-house or external
- video/interactive video

- on-line tutorial
- self-study/step-through guide
- one-to-one training.

- **Characteristics of a good ICT team:**
  - strong leadership
  - appropriate allocation of tasks
  - close monitoring of progress
  - control over resources
  - control over change
  - monitoring of costs.

- **Contents of a code of practice:**
  - responsibilities for use of company hardware
  - responsibilities for use of company software
  - responsibilities for use of data
  - responsibilities for correct use of time
  - responsibilities for use of the Internet or intranet
  - authorisation paths/levels, access rights or job-related
  - security, use of password, identification systems
  - company's implementation of legislation, e.g. the Data Protection Act.

5.1 ICT 5 topics

- **Factors influencing upgrade decisions:**
  - hardware developments
  - software developments
  - task-driven changes
  - organisation ethos changes (such as management changes)
  - software changes (new systems introduced).

- **Evaluation criteria:**
  - an agreed problem specification (i.e. what it is for)
  - functionality requirements
  - how it performs, benchmarking (speed or volume)
  - usability and human/computer interface
  - compatibility with existing software and systems software (and hardware)
  - transferability of data from old system to new
  - robustness (aligned to benchmarking, volatility of product and number of users)
  - user support options available, aligned to users of the system
  - resource requirements (hardware, software and human)
  - upgradability of product
  - portability of product
  - financial issues (one-off costs, on-going maintenance costs).

- **Factors influencing interface design:**
  - use of colour
  - navigation around the system

- amount of text
- size and type (font) of text
- appropriate language
- help available
- error messages/handling
- use of graphics/buttons/icons/pictures/moving images/sounds.

- **Types of human/computer interface:**
  - command line
  - menu-driven
  - graphical user interface.

- **Ways of developing software:**
  - in-house development project
  - outsourcing (externally developed, bespoke)
  - user writes own (normally only simple reports from a larger system)
  - external software house develops to one client's specification then adapts the resulting application for general selling
  - external software house develops a package to an industry standard, to comply with legislation, or to fill a perceived gap in the market where similar businesses all need a similar solution, then markets the package to the target area.

- **Testing methods:**
  - unit – each element, or piece of software, tested with typical, erroneous and extreme cases
  - functional – using data from end to end of the system, testing as many logical paths as possible with contrived data; in a software house situation, this is known as alpha testing
  - end-user testing of functionality – with real data from current data pool; in a software house this is known as beta testing
  - performance and volume testing – using enough data to simulate real life to check timings and ability (robustness) of the system; websites are often tested with many people simultaneously hitting the site to see if it crashes
  - black-box and white-box testing – terms used as alternatives to functional testing and unit testing.

INDEX